Tom's book is  ourney
and generous eft ...... with others. Readers
will find themselves as they follow Tom on his path to
becoming a better Christian man.

- Dr. Gordon W. Stables, III, Professor of Communication and
Journalism, University of Southern California
Editor, *There Are No Politics In Heaven*

With engaging vulnerability, Tom Russo tells his story, which is
uniquely his and, at the same time, has touching points to yours
and mine. Well-written turn-around stories, like this one, are
not just entertaining and inspiring — they are prophetic as they
lightly admonish us to see a better life we can, and should, live.
Tom also shares insightful perspectives on some of life's most
important topics. Enjoy, learn and improve — *There Are No
Politics In Heaven* could well be your turning point.

- Dr. David E. Schroeder, President
Pillar College, Newark, NJ

Raw, vulnerable, telling yet redemptive, hopeful and faith-filled.
This is Tom's story, his God-story, and can be your
inspirational story, too!

- Rev. James Panza, Lead Pastor
Grace Chapel, Bedminster, NJ

Whether it be yin or yang, good or bad, id or ego, life is full of drives and forces; leaving a plethora of choices (big and small) to be made. Knowing Tom for years and seeing, first hand, the impact of some of those choices makes this book even more special to me. *There Are No Politics In Heaven* is the "behind the music" story of a dedicated public servant and, in this well-written tale, you will read about spiritual redemption from pride, gluttony, envy and more. Are you truly interested in service to others over self or is something else behind your actions? Read this book and I am confident you'll find out!

- Adam W. Brewer, Friend and Fellow Manager/Administrator

There Are No Politics In Heaven is a must read for anyone looking for a life-changing experience. I have known Tom Russo and his family for over thirty years. He was my Chief of Staff at a 330-member law enforcement agency. Throughout his career, Tom has consistently demonstrated the importance of service over self, public service over politics. This book is a pleasure to read and is a game-changer for those who are willing to look in the mirror and make the difficult and necessary changes in their life with Tom's wisdom, experience and guidance.

- Sheriff Ed Rochford, Retired, Morris County, NJ

Jesus told His Disciples, "You must be as wise as Serpents and as innocent as Doves." That's great advice for those who follow a path into politics. But Jesus also has life changing advice for us, saying, "I am the Way, the Truth, and the Life." My good friend, Tom Russo, realized that a few years ago, and his book, *There Are No Politics In Heaven,* chronicles Tom's journey of faith. As a fellow "Recovering Politician," I heartily recommend it!

- J.D. Hayworth, Member of Congress, Arizona, 1995-2007

What do you really want out of life? In his frank and honest discussion, Tom Russo shows us how chasing the world's idea of success leaves you unfulfilled. With drive and determination, you can accomplish anything; but will you be happy with what you achieve? Sometimes, you climb the ladder of success only to find out it is leaning against the wrong wall. He went the long route but is finally at the right destination. *There Are No Politics In Heaven* will help you and others avoid these pitfalls. In his look inside the world, Tom learned true inner fulfillment comes from serving others. Learn from the mistakes of others; you don't have time to make them all yourself. It's all in Tom's book. Get your copy today and save yourself a lot of grief!

- Robert H. Springer, Author of *Encouragement Daily*

Basking Ridge, NJ

Thank you for
being a blessing!

Thomas B. Russo Jr.

There Are No Politics In Heaven

A Recovering Politician's Guide to Christian Living

A Memoir by
Thomas S. Russo, Jr.

Edited by Dr. Gordon W. Stables, III
Professor of Communication and Journalism
University of Southern California

Russo Communications, LLC
2019

Table of Contents

About the Author

Mr. Russo currently serves as Town Manager in Newton, NJ, with over eleven years of dedicated service to the County Seat of Sussex County, NJ. Mr. Russo has over 20 years of experience in municipal and county government, as well as the nonprofit sector. His experience includes budgeting, purchasing, human resources, public relations, project oversight, contract negotiations, government relations, economic revitalization & redevelopment, and community relations. Mr. Russo is a competent and confident servant leader; a proven visionary and strategic thinker with highly effective communications and organizational skills.

Mr. Russo previously served as an elected official in two NJ municipalities. He was a Committeeman in Bernards Township from 2014 – 2017. He served as a Councilman, Council Vice President and Council President in Parsippany-Troy Hills Township from 1998 – 2005, earning the distinction as the youngest-ever elected Governing Body member in the history of the Township. Mr. Russo also dedicated time to countless political campaigns from 1992 – 2014, attending several inaugurations and conventions.

He was selected as part of the inaugural class of young elected leaders at the 1st National Young Elected Leaders Conference, Eagleton Institute of Politics, Rutgers University. He was also chosen by the *NJ Herald* in 2009 as one of 40 influential people in Sussex County under the age of 40. Other relevant career experience includes his service as a Fundraising Associate at Far Brook School in Short Hills, NJ; Director of Public Affairs and Information at the Morris County Sheriff's Office in Morristown, NJ; Manager of Development at Chilton Medical Center, Pompton Plains, NJ; Senior Editor, Communications at Organon Pharma USA; and Assistant Township Manager in Randolph, NJ.

Mr. Russo is a member of the New Jersey Municipal Management Association (NJMMA) and is Chairman of the Statewide Insurance Fund, the largest joint public insurance fund in NJ with 80 members across the state. He is a Community Advisory Board member of both Newton Medical Center - Atlantic Health Group and Bristol Glen Independent and Assisted Living Methodist Community. He is also an Executive Committee member of the North Jersey Municipal Employee Benefits Fund (NJMEBF), a consortium of forward-thinking communities which pool resources to effectively manage health insurance costs.

Mr. Russo has a Certified Public Manager (CPM) degree from Fairleigh Dickinson University/State of NJ, a Master of Public Administration (MPA) degree from Seton Hall University, and a Bachelor of Arts (BA) degree in Communication and Political Science from Rutgers, The State University of New Jersey. In addition to undergraduate adjunct teaching at Pillar College in Newark, NJ, Mr. Russo is an adjunct professor in the Department of Political Science and Public Affairs at his alma mater, Seton Hall University, in South Orange, NJ, where he teaches graduate courses on nonprofit management and leadership. He recently published a memoir of his life experiences and how he gave up politics and became a born-again Christian in September 2015. The purpose of his book, *There Are No Politics In Heaven*, is to help men improve their lives with Jesus as their cornerstone.

He currently attends Grace Fellowship Chapel with his family in Bedminster, NJ and serves as a volunteer with Pause Mens Ministries in Basking Ridge, NJ, an organization committed to the recovery and restoration of men through biblical teachings and principles.

He resides in the Basking Ridge section of Bernards Township, NJ with his wife Patricia, the Director of The Children's Corner Preschool at Liberty Corner Presbyterian Church. They have two college-age daughters, Ashley (The Pennsylvania State University) and Krista (Florida State University).

Preface

If you've ever felt lost in your life, with no hope, no options, no direction, and fear so suffocating you couldn't breathe and wanted to die because it would be easier, then this story is your story.

Take a look with me into the mirror of my life, where I faced childhood challenges, rode political highs and lows, achieved external greatness with internal emptiness, confronted the psychological demons within, experienced a religious transformation, and lived to fight another day. Join me on this rollercoaster ride of newfound Christian faith, hope, perseverance, and the ability to change. This is a story about the human condition and our ability to overcome obstacles and find faith bigger than fear, true inner peace and purpose.

It is my sincere hope by reading my story you will learn about yourself and be able to rewrite **your** story. I pray my internal self-reflection of how I experienced my life will allow you the comfort and space to review your life story so you can change direction. **It is never too late.**

If you are a man struggling with issues such as marriage, relationship, family, career, money, faith, and your place in this crazy thing we call life, I am here to suggest a better path and way through Christian faith is just pages away. Thank you for being a part of my journey. I am honored to be part of yours. God Bless.

On a practical note, you will see comments or narration in boxed format (like this) throughout the text of the book. These are my narrator comments that obviously did not occur in real-time during the stories in the book, but are my present-day opinions and thoughts looking back through a very different personal lens. I hope they add some level of value to you with insight, honesty, and humor. Enjoy!

For more information about this book, *There Are No Politics In Heaven*, to schedule Mr. Russo for speaking engagements, or individual leadership coaching and mentoring, please contact him at:

Russo Communications, LLC
c/o Thomas S. Russo, Jr.
trusso@nopoliticsinheaven.com
nopoliticsinheaven.com
973.885.0857

Foreword

I did not know Tom at the "apex" of his political career, I only came to know him soon after he had come into a relationship with his Lord and Savior, Jesus Christ. The Tom I came to know was in what I would term as the "crossover stage". That stage of life where he was working to leave behind the mass of hurt, pain and coping devices he had accumulated in his life and exchange them for a new, Christ-centered life where Tom was no longer the main character or epitome of a game player.

This is not an easy time of life. Tom was faced with the task of leaving his old self behind...a self he knew how to control through confidence and manipulation, and taking on a new life, one that would include things like humility, submission and surrender to Christ.

Tom took on the crossover with a passion. Soaking in the word of God, refocusing his time and attention to loving his wife and family in a new way and surrounding himself with new friends who shared in his faith and encouraged him on his journey to healing. The result is best described in 2 Corinthians 5:17. Tom is a model of that verse.

The new Tom that has emerged is a humble, loving, kind and generous man. He is still successful, a leader in every aspect of his life, but a man willingly guided and directed by the Holy Spirit and led by his faith in Jesus. Tom's story and this book should be an inspiration to each of us to fearlessly do the introspective work needed to find ourselves, and become better husbands, fathers and friends through Christ.

Tom Russo is a remarkable man...a man willing to share his life journey openly, honestly and faithfully. Enjoy his book, *There Are No Politics In Heaven*, and change your life forever.

Dan Bove

President, Pause Ministries

Basking Ridge, NJ

Chapter 1

My Darkest Hour

How did I get here? How did I, the strong, egotistical Type "A" Chief Executive, in September of 2015, wind up on my hands and knees begging to be saved? I felt like the walls were finally closing in on me, and I had no alternatives left. With nowhere to run anymore, this was the end. After 43 years of a life full of shallowness and vapid behavior, of days and nights where I thought I had all the answers, I finally realized I wasn't even asking the right questions, if I was asking any questions at all.

Having all the answers was easy when I was the smartest person in the room. Surrounding myself with those I deemed (unfairly) to be lesser, those who would not have the intellect or worse, the confidence to question me, brought my ego to new heights. And I loved it. My ego and I could do anything, achieve anything, and make others lose sight of what was most important to them.

I was an expert in adaptation, a professional chameleon, a personal charmer, and could move people at will like pawns on a chess board they never knew existed. Their morals and ethics were quickly scattered and lost to the wind, clearly no match for the game I played day in and day out.

Success came at all costs and I not only believed but lived my own press releases – I was a genius and could do no wrong.

How ironic it was the same ego that had blinded everyone from the attractive sycophants across the room, to the political arena I conquered, had made me its first willing victim, blind to the fact I had no moral compass, no religious faith to keep me grounded, no unyielding beliefs, no true core. I was just another unsuccessful member of a large church who had more guilt than any real relationship with God. I needed to end this pain, this self-righteous existence I created for myself while I stepped on the emotional toes of everyone around me to get to the top rung of some superficial ladder. "Why God, why am I this way?", I cried out on the floor, alone in my expansive and well-appointed, now utterly useless office. "I don't want to live this lie anymore – I am tired of being a fraud – please help me and I vow to change my ways if you will show me how. I don't have the answers anymore."

It was at that moment a never before experienced sense of calm came through every fiber of my being. With no one but me in the room, it was then I heard a voice say, "Tom…it's time."

Chapter 2

The Womb Was Warm

I was born in 1972 at Chilton Memorial Hospital (now an Atlantic Health Medical Center) in Pompton Plains, NJ. My initial childhood years through the age of 7 were spent in Lincoln Park, NJ in a non-descript section of the flood-prone community. Those years seemed simple back then. Family members lived near-by and I remember a lot of happiness and connectivity to them. I used to always have a smile on my face and a microphone (real or imaginary) nearby. My being named after my Dad and being the family's baby boy had heartened me with a great attention level like an actor on a stage. It came naturally and without any self-conscious fear of disapproval from those around me. I think I was the entertainment for the family back then, in some ways, I still am today.

There was a big supermarket in town not too far from where we lived, and I used to do a belly dance for the female cashiers at the store. Not sure in hindsight how appropriate that was while people were waiting to pay for their milk and eggs; nevertheless, I seemed to make people smile during their dreary retail existence, an escape from the daily minutia they endured.

I enjoyed making others smile; I made it a point to bring that sort of simple joy to the people around me, and I reveled in the positive attention they gave me in return. It's human nature to want to be liked, to be applauded and encouraged, and as children we are awarded this kindness without judgment, bias or criticism found when the golden years of innocence finally fade and reality hits you like the fists of a school-yard bully.

There was a Corner Store in town not too far from our house where I learned to love comic books. My mother encouraged my reading endeavors and comics were pretty simple reads back then, and I took the time to absorb all those wonderful stories of heroes and villains, of good vs. evil. That is how my do-gooder mentality started. What a blissful feeling it was to know as a child that good would always win out, boy gets girl, and your favorite hero would escape the clutches of evil, even though your heart pounded in anxiety until you reached the next page and discovered the villain would be overconfident and miss some sort of detail our hero would exploit to victory! In time, that unintended escape into the world of comic book reality would provide me with a useful lesson I never thought I'd need to revisit.

We grew up happy as lower middle class and were comfortable enough to have no idea what the value of that label intended. Dad was gainfully employed as a truck driver and Mom was a stay-at-home Mom. My sister was 6 years older than me and we were a typical Italian Catholic family with aunts and uncles and cousins all over northern NJ and lots of food and laughter. All was good. And then in 1979, when we moved to Parsippany, things changed.

Chapter 3

Fat Is Not Where It's At

When we moved to the brown bi-level home in Lake Parsippany, I had lots of mixed emotions. I think as a child you go along for the emotional roller coaster ride of moving, not knowing what your new life will look like, hoping your parents know what the heck they are doing to your formerly perfectly defined world, trusting as only a child in the prime of their innocence could that they were taking you by the hand and leading you to a new, exciting beginning in an unknown land. Youth makes new places, if only a short distance away, albeit in the same state, seem like a world apart.

There was definite sadness about leaving behind familiar friends and surroundings, and yes, the comic book store, my first and beloved familiar escape that would become a fond memory of my simple, happy childhood existence. But there was a nicer house in a friendly-looking neighborhood on the horizon, so I gave it a shot, willing myself to think I had a choice in the matter of the greatest upheaval in my short life I had ever experienced.

The timing of the move was more of a challenge, however. Moving mid-year of 1st grade was a bit of bad timing; making new friends quickly, sharing stories and lunches needed to become the new normal if I was going to survive, and I was fortunate to befriend several kids that lived in close proximity to our house and the elementary school.

Back then you walked to and from school without much worry (or so I thought, more on that later). Parents didn't fret about their child being stolen from the roadway – non-descript vans were not labeled suspicious and we knew they didn't contain imaginary candy or puppies. Neighbors were comprised of the typical nuclear family units and everyone kept a watchful eye out for the local kids without simply being asked because it was the right thing to do. The houses were close together and walking and playing around the neighborhood or riding bikes for hours upon end were common activities for myself and many other kids.

It's funny, as I sit here and type this book at my home in Basking Ridge, NJ, I think about how little activity occurs in the streets around me today. There are times it feels more like a movie set than an actual neighborhood. Welcome to The Russo Show, formerly The Truman Show.

Like many Italian Catholics, I went through a religious education program, CCD, which I begrudgingly attended at St. Christopher's RC Church in town.

I can't say I remember much about the program or teachings, though I schlepped my way there without fail which I think made me a good Catholic boy in an upstanding Catholic family. I was born into the tribe and my religious script was already written, published, and sold with a second edition on the way before you could wrap your head around faith or what it truly meant to have a fulfilling and, more importantly, willing relationship with God. Like death and taxes, it seemed back then like it was just something you had to do. In Lake Parsippany Elementary School, I was a good student, spending a lot of time in the school library reading and absorbing stories, a new safe place to go with my uncertain new life.

A step up from comics in a way – libraries will be a common thread throughout this book, maybe you are even reading this book in one right now!

I loved the escapism and sense of wonder and awe found in fiction books. I also used to do the pledge of allegiance on the school p.a. system, a natural extension of my pseudo-microphone hogging childhood days in Lincoln Park.

Always looking for positive, ego-boosting attention and what better way to achieve this harmless goal, that innocent love for a reserved time slot every morning or afternoon, where my voice would boom above the heads of not only my peers, but teachers as well, portraying every ounce of confidence and pure elation of knowing that everyone, and I mean, *everyone* could hear me. There was no doubt in my mind that I was not only heard, but by association, my peers listened and followed my lead as I instructed them when to stand, what words to repeat, and finally, when they were allowed to take their seat. Of course, I had a strict regimen to follow and it would have meant dire consequences I could not bear if I strayed from the script, but the dream of leading my peers and those in positions of higher authority with my voice was born and firmly rooted in my core.

When WHTZ 100.3-FM, Z-100, was launched in New York City, their on-air "Morning Zoo" announcers made stops around schools for promotional endeavors and I remember meeting them and being in awe of people whose voices I heard on the radio.

The love of music I gained from my father, whose influence had become increasingly prevalent since our upheaval, definitely impacted me as I was in the presence of radio personalities Captain Kevin, Jack the Whack, and Professor Jonathan B. Bell. I saw how the kids, and adults, treated them and admired the guffawing and adulation. Maybe being famous and popular was something worth aspiring to, I wondered. Even then, with very little understanding of my subconscious or ego, I was nothing if not motivated to pursue a path that would lead me to external greatness.

Back then there was a program at school called "GRO" or Gifted Reach Out. I tested for it initially but was unable to make the cut of higher intellect. Even at that age, I was disappointed at my lack of ability. I rarely tried something I could not succeed in, hence why you have not read about my attempting to excel at sports yet. Failing was not something I did well and my need to excel, to be different, to attain a label as one of the *gifted*, gave me drive. I felt a lack within myself I needed to fulfill, and it made me hungry for every ounce of greatness, every last morsel of approval I could find. Eventually I would realize no matter what I was given, no matter what I earned, this hunger would be impossible to satiate.

A couple of years later I was re-tested and made this very small group of brainiacs. Mission accomplished! The knowledge I was above average or outside the norm in a good way came over me like a tidal wave, drowning out any negative aspects I would come to endure. My best friend and local neighborhood buddy Gordon was in the program (more on him later) since its inception and I was now fortunate to do activities with him and things other kids didn't get to do including some version of a rudimentary newsletter for publication.

The GRO program was a mixed blessing. Doing newsletters is something I have done throughout my career and still do to this very day. However, this great honor set the stage for thinking I was smarter than everyone else. In hindsight, no, I was not the best and I did not do everything the right way. The wave of pride I rode for many years would eventually break and toss me into a riptide I could not fight my way out of...alone.

In spite of the academic success, I faced dark moments, too. As time progressed during these early developmental years, I started to gain weight. Slowly at first like most people, but over time it just seemed to catch up to me.

When you are "Tom-Tom" or "Junior" or "Tom Jr." you didn't mind such terms of endearment for they were said with love. When in the real world you were often ridiculed, called less than loving names, and made fun of for being overweight; when the success or failure of the all-important tug-of-war game consistently and painfully revolved around your girth and which team picked you (last) to be the anchor. Or when you had your Halloween costumes ridiculed because maybe they weren't as stylish or unique as those found on others; it left an indelible scar on my character and soul. This was a cruel world, I thought at the time. Kids suck. I made people laugh, I could engage them in conversation about books or sports, but it always came with opportunities for others to judge me because of my obesity or attire or income status. Or all of the above. The same judgment I would use later in life to judge others.

There was one time the bullying came to a head when I was walking home from school, for lunch, and I made it to the end of my street but found myself being physically attacked and pushed around like a rag doll by a neighborhood thug.

My Dad was home that day (not sure why) and he ran all the way from our end of the street to the other end where my experience in being bullied took a different, painful turn.

I wish I had the ability to fight back physically but I wasn't actually very strong, despite what my classmates believed about weight and power in tug-of-war. My Dad was able to remove the thug off of me and we made our way home. I was glad my Dad saved me from the torture and humiliation but wondered if I was supposed to handle it on my own? If I could not protect myself, did I deserve to be mistreated? Allowing myself to let others save me, to handle my problems, to enable me to avoid discovering a better way to manage the painful onslaught of judgment without provocation brought me to question my own self-worth. *What was I worth?* Those thoughts would haunt me for years to come.

With the bullying clearly at the forefront of my days in school, I once again immersed myself in studies and mental pursuits to escape the pain. I dutifully performed activities as part of the School Safety Patrol and enjoyed my taste of leadership and responsibility.

I found myself following current events more and more on television at the time, too, either as an escape or just because the news always was on at home. President Ronald Reagan and NJ Governor Tom Kean, Sr. were always speaking about something on television and it seemed from what I could gather most people liked them.

Hmmm, I thought, I could learn more about what they are talking about and people would like me, too? So, I did what Tom normally did and dove headfirst into books and magazines on things most of my peers could have cared less about.

While students were more worried about sports or cartoons, I found myself analyzing electoral college maps and whether Florida was indeed a blue or red state. Politicians seemed cool and popular. They were people who got things done! No one would dare pick them last for sports. In fact, people seemed to be in a frenzy just to be on their team. They led and were accepted as undisputed captains of the political playground and much like the kids who pretended to be friendly when I was finally given my long-awaited turn to choose a team, the public jumped to be a part of their battles with nothing short of a unified chorus asking, "how high, sir?"

I wanted to be *that* type of person to invoke such an admirable following of the masses more than I had ever wanted anything else. With this new dream in mind, and the smarts to follow through, the political bug was born. It wasn't as good as getting bitten by a radioactive spider, but it would have to do.

When I got to middle school, emotional challenges continued. Nobody really prepared me for the transition to this bigger school farther away from home and the safety of the nest my parents created. Back then Brooklawn Middle School was a Junior High, so only grades 7 and 8 were there. Sort of a brief stop before you made it to the big leagues of high school at Parsippany Hills (PHHS). I *hated* my time at Brooklawn.

A nice school for sure, but I did not fit in. I missed the simplicity and proximity of the elementary school and the fact I worked my way up to be endeared by teachers and academically accomplished. I was now a stranger in a strange land, and it sucked. Not only that, but with financial stressors at home coupled with the stressors of my new school, my weight started to balloon. I think I was born with a smile on my face but not much of a metabolism.

I used to hide my emotional battles in food – snacks at home, remnants of other people's lunches at school. When they were done eating in the cafeteria at lunchtime my work was just beginning, as extra fries, snacks, and unfinished ice cream sundaes came my way like I was a human garbage disposal. Do you want fries with that – well yes, I do!

My initial high school years were not much better. PHHS was a big campus where my sister had graduated from in 1984, only a few years before my initial start in the fall of 1986. My sister was a better student than I was and had built a lot of rapport with many teachers and counselors at the school so that in a way helped pave my start at the mothership of Parsippany public schools.

My high school years can be broken down into 2 vastly different segments – the fat years of Freshman and Sophomore years and the Stud-mode years of Junior and Senior years. The nexus between the two is quite a doozy. *Who knew starvation tasted so good?*

Chapter 4

A Lot of U's But
What About Me?

Freshman year of high school was like being thrown into the deep end of the pool without knowing exactly how to swim. And trust me, I was not a great swimmer. My reputation as an anchor continued to precede me in more ways than one and my buoyancy was boosted about as much as my self-esteem. Needless to say, I sunk.

I struggled through my classes while trying my best. Once a self-proclaimed brainiac, I now felt void of any hope that promised the bright, successful future I had dreamt of since my comic book store youth. I was a failure and a pariah; power did not come to those who were treated as targets rather than human beings. I became involved in some activities but did not assimilate in the same fashion as other kids did. When I was in elementary school all the kids looked and acted the same. As I went to middle school, the circle expanded so there were kids of all shapes, sizes, ethnic backgrounds and income levels.

When I was in high school my freshman year, it was like an explosion of color, sights, sounds and smells (who can forget the ever-popular outdoor smoking lounge or as it was affectionately called, the scrounge lounge?). I was more abnormal than ever, feeling the stress of the harsh scrutiny my ever-increasing waist size attracted. This negative attention over the Fat Tom years compounded into one giant chip super-glued to my shoulder.

My sophomore year experience was not much better. All I did was struggle to fit in and find my way. All I did was eat myself to a larger existence of portly and husky clothing. And although the bullying was not the same as it was at the playground of Lake Parsippany Elementary School, it was more covert and sinister. It was almost easier when people said nasty or stupid things to your face, at least you knew where they stood with you. But in high school, it was done behind your back. The whispers in the hallway as you walked past, or as they walked past you while you stood at your locker just waiting for the minutes to tick by, so you could get out of Dodge.

In some ways, it was more painful to not know; to let your own mind take half-whispered words, filling in the blanks with the worst your own mind could and already had imagined. But hey, degrading myself was second nature at this point.

Kids were cruel I continued to think, nothing changed.

But I noticed there were two things that were the great equalizers in high school – either you had to be academically gifted (alas, my legendary GRO elementary school days were quite far behind me according to my lackluster report cards) or you had to be a kick-ass athlete of some kind.

At Parsippany Hills, the football team was not competitive, so the boy sports that seemed to attract the most attention (and girls) were soccer and baseball. As someone who had participated for many years in one of the two organized little league programs in town, I thought high school baseball was worth the try. Boy was I wrong.

I had heard of something called "carb loading" and I thought it meant you ate a ton of carbs before any rigorous activity, so you could have these awesome bursts of strength, energy and speed (like a comic book superhero, nice!). Well, I didn't pay attention to the part where they teach you that carb loading does NOT occur 30 minutes before the activity. Whoops. So, it was tryout time for the baseball team in the spring of my sophomore year of high school.

My Dad was kind enough to take me to the tryouts at the gymnasium. I had just eaten a ton of pasta right before the tryouts, so I was quite confident with my Mizuno first baseman's glove and my stomach full of Ronzoni I was going to kill it!

Mangia bene my butt. *No wonder Alfred had never brought Batman a dish of pasta before he jumped into the Batmobile.*

Instead the tryouts killed me as I think I lasted less than 20 minutes, if that. Don Mattingly I wasn't.

As the calisthenics and exercises were just beginning, I could feel the gravity of the situation, or the gravity of pasta and sauce working its way from my stomach to throat, worsen. I needed to leave, and I needed to leave right then and there.

I don't believe my Dad was too thrilled, but he didn't have much of a choice in the matter as I insisted it was time to go. Tryouts went on without me and I didn't make the team (duh). My father was forced to save me, yet again, adding to what I felt was the growing disappointment to his one and only namesake. His approval was even much further away now. I loved my mother and the nurturing she gave me, a true matriarch of the family.

I mean, let's face it, in Italian families the woman, quiet as they may be at times, was the real ruler of the roost. She along with my grandmothers gave me all the love I'd ever need, but my father's love and approval, that was something I felt I had to earn on a daily basis. Once again, I felt too powerless to even attain that, a victim of my own inability to last a mere 20 minutes at high school baseball tryouts. Pathetic. We got back to the previously aforementioned brown bi-level.

I made my way up the steps, completely dejected and embarrassed as I had failed on my mission for baseball immortality and greatness, or at least, high school popularity, and I did what came naturally.

I threw up.

Yes, right off the side of the front steps of the house. Fan-friggin-tastic in all its red Ronzoni glory. So much for carb loading.

But here is where the story got interesting. Before I made it through the front door, I decided I was not going to be that fat kid anymore. I vowed I would do whatever it took to lose the mound of weight and belly fat so humiliation would never be an everyday part of my miserable existence.

Power did not come from dreaming, it came from putting on a mask to hide your identity and insecurities. Good or bad, right or wrong, I would find a way to get the love, respect, fame, and fortune I knew I deserved if it was the last thing I did in this short and, up to that moment, miserable life. I was going to be the one thing they never saw coming, a chameleon. It was at that moment I used my drive and determination to come up with a game plan for success and hero-like glory and victory would be mine!

They would rue the day they made fun of Fat Tom.

Now it was time for stud-mode! Or more like, starvation mode. What do you do when you spent your life overeating and gaining a ton of weight? You either exercise like a fiend or drastically cut back on caloric intake.

I would talk more about insulin, cortisol, intermittent fasting, gluten-free and low carb, but hey, this was years before that science really took off; back then it was more like the little red calorie book, ever have one of those?

My choice was clear – I would do both! Clearly this would accelerate the process. Screw the laziness of the past, overachieving Tom was back, baby! I started that spring with my new regiment of low calories and high intensity exercise. Instead of triangular-shaped cheese covered nacho chips being my friend, the exercise bike got most of my attention.

During New York Rangers hockey games and evening game shows, my butt was glued to that bike as much as pine tar to George Brett's infamous bat. There was one Saturday where I think I rode for 9 hours straight.

Clearly, I was motivated. But was it for health reasons or positive attention? So, I could look good on television when President Reagan shook my hand, congratulating me on being the youngest yet greatest politician he'd ever seen, since, well, himself? Nevertheless, the results were astounding. While other kids were off for the summer going on vacations or doing other things, I was obsessing over my weight loss. Weighing myself daily, monitoring my progress like brokers track the stock ticker. The goal was to lose 100 lbs. by the time I started my junior year of high school.

And I achieved my goal. I needed a new wardrobe and entered my third year of high school ready to conquer the world.

And on the first day, people said...*who are you?* Not exactly the reaction I was hoping for but not bad either. I eagerly explained to the masses that it was I, the formerly Fat Tom, who was now evolved into a much studlier version of himself, ready for the obvious adulation and attention (ahem...girls!) that must be forthcoming.

The great thing was I lost the weight. The sad thing was I lost myself in the process, as I traded one cruel reality for another. The bullying and negative comments ceased to exist.

They were replaced with the reality that society judges us by the shell of ourselves, what we present to the world on the outside (attire, charm, pseudo-interesting personality, etc.), not by the content of your character. I was still the same fun-loving Tom, the guy with the smile and intellect, but now society liked me, they really, really liked me. And that was the most important thing in the world to me. I pushed aside my societal sadness and moved forward, chin up and shoulders back!

I was ready to take on those fickle, shallow pretenders and chart my own course. The only question that remained was, who would be the first to join *my* team?

Now, with less weight in tow, my junior and senior years were full of confidence, activities, popularity and happiness. Never mind I was falling asleep in classes because I had no energy from continuing to starve myself. Who cared! Who needed sleep, sleep was for the weak. Adulation was far more important! If the price for being thin was being sent to the principal's office because I was asleep in English class, then so be it! Every time I fell asleep, I awoke to thin thoughts in a thin reality. It was the most earth-shattering validation I had ever experienced, and it was more addictive than any drug (or nacho snack) I could imagine.

I also spent my lunch periods in the safety of the high school library. Once again, books and magazines and quiet time were safe havens away from people and their judgment, food and their calories. As long as I had my sugarless gum in tow, which I used to give to kids around me like I was a drug pusher selling crack, I was good to go!

In high school I had continued my interest in politics and current events and learned the art of campaign management. My greatest childhood friend, Gordon, who had stuck with me through thick and thin (literally and figuratively), ran for class office. I worked on the campaign posters and speech and he won. Gordon became the likeable bridge amongst all groups in our class and he won in a landslide. I felt great pride in his accomplishment and wondered if being behind the scenes was better (and safer) for me?

I continued to assist others as they successfully ran for various class offices. When I decided hey what about me and ran for class office, I was unsuccessful but took it as an important life lesson that sometimes you win, sometimes you lose, and immersed myself in so many activities that in my senior year I received an inaugural scholarship named after the first principal of the high school.

My hard work paid off and I was finally recognized. I learned I did not need a title to stand out to be successful or helpful. (Sadly, I would see that lesson become a recurring theme that didn't dissipate until that fateful moment in my office in September 2015).

I became active in the Forensics program and learned the art of extemporaneous speaking. Being given a current events topic and having a very brief amount of time to research the topic with information you needed to have already collected and filed, write or outline a speech and present it without notes to multiple judges became a great way for a kid who was previously stuck in his own shell and, an underachiever, to learn the art of being outgoing and persuasive and one of the truly most important life skills, public speaking. I was very successful with this and other activities which would become the foundation for future academic, professional and political success. Each win, each round of applause and every smile in my direction made me work harder; to excel on this new-found path to acceptance and greatness. If this road was that of the less traveled, it was for me. If there was ever a question in my mind before, I now knew public speaking and engagement were the answers.

I was also chosen to do the morning and afternoon announcement on the p.a. system – sound familiar? Once again, my booming voice was dictating the comings and goings and happenings for the masses in a school. Each morning I would leave my class earlier and earlier, telling my teacher that Mr. Saul Goodman (the activities coordinator) needed me for some x-y-z project.

Not true, mind you, but it gave me the ability to have free will and manage my time and announcement schedule as I saw fit.

When it came time to work on colleges, I chose ones I heard had good political science programs. I was able to get into George Mason University (GMU) in Fairfax, VA where Gordon was going. He was one of the top debaters in high school in NJ at the time (if not the country) and was going to debate at GMU. Since I had always admired Gordon for his intellect (he was part of the inaugural GRO program at Lake Parsippany Elementary School and smarter than I would ever be) and debate success I decided to follow him to GMU. It also didn't hurt to keep just one piece of home near me on this new journey. Not many people in my family had ever traveled away so far from the nest. It was a shock to them, but I knew with Gordon on my side, my dogged determination to succeed and brains to spare I would be right at home in no time.

I had the choice of being on the Forensics Team or Debate Team at GMU and decided to try something different and be on the Debate Team.

That was a great choice for me as not only were we one of the best teams in the country and I got to travel to different colleges to compete, I would be able to spend more time with Gordon while I made some other close friends (I still keep in touch with them to this day).

In my second year at George Mason I turned down the opportunity to be a part of the Debate Team once again in order to earn some spending money at, you guessed it, the college library. It was there I first learned of this amazing NJ shore town called Spring Lake (which would then become my favorite spot in NJ for sun and fun – who knew I would discover this great place in NJ while I was sitting in a library reading magazines in Fairfax, VA?).

My grades were up. My weight was down. Life was good. Until, I realized the college experience of northern Virginia was financially challenging for my parents and I decided to transition to Rutgers College at Rutgers University-New Brunswick, NJ. Back to the nest where comfort and routine surrounded me.

Ironically, I was not good enough to get into Rutgers College the first time I applied in high school, but I didn't let that stop me as I came home to live, worked at my old high school job of the video rental store, spent time with my girlfriend, and commuted to Rutgers. I graduated in May of 1994 with my dual bachelor's degree in Political Science and Communication and had an important decision to make. I knew I wanted to go into politics, so was I going to be another lawyer, another shark in a sea of these creatures in politics and go to law school? Or was I going to chart my own path and go for a Master's in Public Administration degree from Seton Hall University? I chose the latter and it was one of the best life decisions I ever made. Political glory here I come!

Chapter 5

Council Boy Pays His Dues

While I was attending graduate school commuting back and forth to Seton Hall University, I became immersed in local politics in Parsippany, a humble and valuable beginning. I ran for Republican County Committee against an incumbent and decided I would put my campaign skills to use once again with a simple tried and true strategy, phone calls and a mailer. I noticed most people who ran for the County Committee positions (like political block captains) just held onto them for years because no one else was interested in the poorly publicized but important party machine positions. My County Committeeman had gotten comfortable in his District 13 seat of limited but admirable power and I intended to give him a run for his money. The purpose of the County Committee was to generate votes during election time, register new voters when people moved into your area of town, stay current on town happenings and issues that might impact your neighborhood, and be available to vote at conventions when an officeholder leaves for one reason or another.

A conduit between the political party and voters; a friendly, trustworthy face often seen at the gas station, grocery store, church, and town functions and events. In spite of the challenge of managing work, school, a steady relationship, and the campaign, it was a wonderful opportunity for a young person like me to get his fill of the first stage of politics.

Winning the election was a great stepping-stone for my political endeavors and certainly a fulfilling ego-boost. Not to mention the position came with the title Honorable. You better believe every time I got a piece of mail and saw Hon. Thomas S. Russo, Jr., my insides did the most comical ego dance I could imagine. While I felt grateful for all the support and proud of the hard work I put in, I couldn't help but have a slight grin thinking, "Honorable...your damn straight I am!"

Beyond County Committee and the local Republican Club, I knew it was important for me to get involved with local political campaigns as I had done in high school. Whether it was for local, county or state offices, I knew getting my name and face out there was important for my future success. A pivotal moment in this journey came in 1995 when a good friend of mine decided to run for Town Council against the political machine at the time and several well-known, entrenched incumbents.

The opportunity was given to me to run this unconventional campaign on a shoe-string budget. With the candidate being a graduate of the other high school in town (Parsippany High) and a fairly well-known local businessman, it presented an opportunity to take things I learned in high school and my own County Committee race and apply them to real-world politics.

Alongside the candidate and I was the campaign treasurer who appropriately managed our limited funds for election law compliance. It was a thrill to be able to design campaign flyers, fundraising materials, letters, signs, buttons, bumper stickers and the like. Even though the opponents were far more well-known and had a great deal more funding, we did our best to keep up with the barrage of campaign marketing. When they sent out 4-color glossy mailers, we responded with a respectable 2-color piece. When they staked their claim to the yards of supporters and grassy main streets with fancy lawn signs, we held our own with cheaper but equally, if not more, effective signs that frustrated the incumbents to no end. The campaign was like a sandbox for me and I got to play in it every day. On primary election day in June, my candidate was one of the top three vote getters, joining one other newcomer in defeating two of the incumbents while a third incumbent survived.

I was able to run the fall campaign for this new hybrid ticket of Republican Council candidates as they went on to victory in November. I started to build up a nice reputation as an organized person who could effectively manage people and resources towards a clearly defined goal or mission (skills that would be necessary as I pursued a full-time municipal government career later on in life).

While I was becoming the next Lee Atwater, I was taking my MPA classes at Seton Hall from great professors who were experts in the field of government and nonprofit management and I worked on campus as a graduate assistant in the Center for Public Service, the department which housed the MPA degree program I was attending. I was a busy boy! Talk about synergy – I got to interact with students and professors and university leadership all day long and take classes at night. I was paid a stipend and relished being a resource for the professors of the department while earning my degree. It felt good to be accepted and even needed for my natural talent and ideal experience in the field. A job I loved, minimum wage payment, and a free master's degree? Genius! The MPA degree would take two years to complete full-time and be mine in the spring of 1996. I graduated with a 3.96 GPA (one darn B+) and loved every minute of it.

The small, intimate feel of the lush South Orange campus of this Catholic university suited my personality so much better than the large, impersonal city feel of public state university Rutgers. The thought of getting lost amongst the crowd with no way to stand out was not my idea of higher education and left me wanting for the individual opportunities Seton Hall offered.

A smaller, more personal surrounding gave me the comfort of home in away; to assimilate, stand out comfortably, and the freedom to be recognized not only as Tommy Russo but as part of a family, both within the department and the University. I spent many hours in the beautiful chapel on campus, wondering what my future would look like, asking God to help guide my decision-making while I stared at the majestic altar and colorful stained-glass windows. Sometimes with happy thoughts, sometimes with fear of the future.

With no clear mentor at that point to help me work through the angst of my 20's, I found the chapel, much like the library, to be a safe place to escape the sudden halts, twists and turns life placed in front of me. While both the library and the chapel gave me peace and solitude, each fed my mind and soul differently making the weight of the world far less a burden to bear alone.

Things in general were moving forward. I was achieving academic success at Seton Hall and I was becoming a rising super-star in Parsippany politics. Hard work and perseverance were indeed paying off.

As recognition for my hard work during the Parsippany campaign I was able to secure a spot on the Zoning Board of Adjustment, a coveted role as far as volunteer positions were concerned. The opportunity to learn first-hand about how government actually works, especially as it related to land-use matters and construction projects, was a fantastic learning experience. Classes in college and grad school were great; but reviewing plans and listening to testimony and members of the public weigh-in on applications was even better. This was not an environment for people-pleasers or flip-floppers; the easily influenced or the bleeding hearts. It was one of carefully weighed decisions which would affect both residents and businesses alike. I could only vote my conscience and hope to feel comfortable in my decisions while trying not to fall asleep those long meeting nights. I wanted to help, do good for others, and be seen as respectful and fair. The idealist in my head told me this was how I would get respect in return. I listened more than I talked and absorbed as much first-hand information during my tenure. I didn't need to be the center of attention, I needed to focus on what I was doing.

Opening my mouth was not worth the risk of being labeled a fool, so until I had something informed to say, mum was the word. I was grateful my campaign endeavors transferred into a volunteer position in the town I grew up in, further solidifying my path towards greatness.

When 1997 rolled around, after having spent many nights going to Council meetings (not televised or streamed online back then) and socializing with the politicos at dinners and fundraisers, I decided, "hey, if they can do it, I can do it, too!" I made the decision to run for Town Council myself. I figured I had nothing to lose. I was still living home with my parents, was in a good relationship, and had a great new pair of black Rockport dress shoes I was ready to wear-out while going door-to-door. Parsippany was a large town made up of quite a number of diverse neighborhoods, so I figured I knew a lot of people on my side of town having gone to elementary school, middle school, and high school on the Lake Parsippany side. This would give me an opportunity to re-connect with people I graduated with (and their parents) as well as make new friends and acquaintances throughout the 25-square mile metropolis of 50,000 residents.

And since my friend's campaign two-years prior, with him running as a 31-year old candidate, me running at age 24 seemed a logical progression of the political transformation of the local party. Or at least a good ego trip for me.

One of the best parts of running was how insane it made some of the old-timers in the political world. They could not comprehend how young our party was becoming and how they could not control us young whipper-snappers. We were young and hungry and full of ideas and energy. Before change was cool, we were the change agents. Several of the powers-that-be tried to get me to not run for this local office, instead offering me delusions of grandeur of future volunteer or paid positions here or there.

Yawn.

This was the classic story of the haves and have nots, I told myself. I was not going to be diminished with empty promises. I knew that nothing sounded as good to me as being "Councilman Russo" so I politely refused and marched onward and upward.

Well, maybe not so politely as I was full of piss and vinegar back then and let my ego drive those conversations into the "I'm going to win…and you have to figure out who is going to lose on your end" ground.

Because of my braggadocio, I was able to secure a spot on a ticket with a well-known male Council incumbent who was running for Mayor and a female newcomer who was running for one of the two available Council seats. With me filling the 2nd Council slot, the ticket was locked and loaded, and we were off and running!

Or at least walking. And walking. And walking some more.

I met so many nice people going door-to-door. And so many weird ones, too. It was a great exercise, both physically and mentally, knocking on someone's door, or ringing their house bell, not knowing what exactly was going to be thrown at you – verbally or otherwise.

There were houses where I got invited in for coffee to sit down and discuss local issues.

There were houses where I got chased away, either by the resident or the dog, or both.

There were houses where homeowners or renters didn't think to change or modify their attire, with some more scantily clad than others. Strange.

One of the smartest things I did during the door-to-door activities actually was observe my surroundings as I entered the property. What kind of cars did they drive? What kind of bumper stickers were on those vehicles? Did they have any flags or outdoor displays that would indicate anything personal about them like favorite sports teams or colleges? You would be surprised how many people ran for office and didn't observe those things. I made sure, however, by the time I got to the door, I was prepared with a mental arsenal of material to throw at them in order to garner their vote and support. More often than not, it seemed to work.

The real joy of the campaign for me was being able to spend hours with my Dad during a plethora of diverse activities, as my campaign and the other previous campaigns, became opportunities for me and him to connect at a greater level of friendship and camaraderie.

My mother, the excellent judge of character and life she was, was not a fan of the political cesspool I was now swimming in and kept her distance. The scores of others who volunteered countless hours, to make phone calls, coordinate fundraisers, put up lawn signs, or go door-to-door, made the campaign way too much fun. The campaign was more than that – it became a family. The meetings, functions, dinners, arguments, etc., were all built upon mutual respect and goal-achievement (victory).

All was not hunky dory, however. During one debate, one of my opponents started down a verbal path of how he and his running mate were "real men" because they were married, had kids, paid property taxes, etc. – all veiled but not so veiled digs at a 24-year old whipper-snapper (moi) who lived at home with his parents and thought he could rule the world. The insinuation of course was that I could not understand the difficulties of family life and town responsibilities. Staying calm and grabbing hold of some of the more reactionary responses my ego wanted to let fly, I found just a wee bit of joy in turning the tables and frustrating them with my off-the-cuff thoughtful response. As a young but dedicated member of the community, one who had grown up with a front row seat to many of the issues we debated today, I would be the perfect person to represent the next generation of residents who wanted a better Parsippany.

While others in my generation were being passive and letting life pass them by, I was choosing to be active, to have my voice be heard as a clarion call for change. Boom. If I could have dropped the mic, I would have. Comments about me being a future mayor soon filled the room, and I walked away from the evening victorious for at least holding my own to a draw, if not victory.

On the primary election night in June, my Council running mate was the clear victor and I actually lost along with my mayoral candidate. As a due formality, however, since the election results were so close, he and I asked the judge in Morristown, NJ for a recount which was respectfully granted. I had already resigned myself to the loss and felt the pain of defeat all the way down to my miserable core. After being so self-assured, so confident in my ability to be a part of a small but determined front who would make changes in a town that was full to the brim of the same tired politics year after year, losing the primary was a blow to my ego and pride I had never felt before. I had romanticized the outcome of the election many times over the past few months; sometimes winning by a hair, others by a landslide, but always the same reaction, immeasurable joy.

The realization it would always be my destiny to stay behind the scenes quickly settled in right next to a large helping of self-blame. What could I have done differently? I didn't have answers at that time. I had let everyone down. I had chosen the wrong path and that was one extraordinarily difficult pill to swallow.

Funny how quickly life changes direction...

I will never forget the moment as I was working at a private school in Short Hills, NJ at the time doing fundraising (more on my career zigs and zags later), when my sister Lisa called me to tell me I won the recount and was victorious in my primary Council campaign! I had lost by ten and now I won by 7! I was the phoenix and rose from the ashes! I was back, baby! What an interesting lesson in humility and patience God had placed in front of me. Holy mixed messages, Batman!

Sometimes I wonder what life would have been like if the recount wasn't granted, or if the numbers didn't change, my life would have been very different personally, professionally and politically. I could have given up running campaigns and followed in the footsteps of my childhood idol, Jerry Lewis. Being a gifted entertainer and someone who raised money for charity, would have fulfilled my genuine will and desire to help people. It would have also put me in closer proximity to a microphone. Entertainment could surely rival politics and leadership qualities were most definitely transferrable – hence why President Reagan was so captivating.

Alas, victory was mine! My mayoral candidate was not successful in his recount and another hybrid Republican ticket for the fall was created with my Council running mate and I selected along with the mayoral candidate from the opposing side of the GOP.

In the November election, my Council running mate and I were elected while the voters chose the Democrat mayoral candidate, thus maintaining split government in Parsippany with checks and balances on both sides (an all-GOP legislative body and Democrat chief executive).

I was sworn into office on January 1, 1998 and my elected political career was zooming ahead. Or so I thought. I soon learned running for office (or running campaigns for that matter) was completely different than actually serving on a legislative body. It wasn't that it was over my head; but going door-to-door and putting up campaign lawn signs is nowhere near as important or intimidating as sitting up on a dais looking over ordinances and resolutions which impact the lives and quality of life of 50,000 people.

I took my time, asked questions when appropriate, and made reasoned decisions after listening to both sides of every issue. I didn't let my party affiliation dictate anything either as I respected the voters who elected the Democrat for mayor and made my decisions based on what was best for the town I grew up in and not for one political party over another.

The *Daily Record* newspaper ran a story in the spring on me with the headline "Council Boy Pays His Dues". The picture was me as the youngest elected official along with one of the other councilmen who was the oldest. I wasn't too thrilled with the headline initially when I picked up the paper at the newspaper box at the Parsippany post office early that morning. In fact, I was so pissed I paid for one newspaper and took a dozen out of the box.

I drove over to my new girlfriend's house and showed her the story. The "Council Boy" moniker was from a quote from one of the old timers in town, not exactly said with love and affection I am certain. But the title stuck, and I actually used it as motivation to show the old guard that with my college degree and Masters, and with all the excitement and energy I was bringing to the table, that my tenure on the Governing Body of my hometown would be meaningful and worthwhile. And I was proven to be correct.

After I finished discussing the article with my significant other, I actually went back to the newspaper box at the post office and finished putting in quarters to cover the cost of the actual amount of newspapers I took – I didn't want the paper boy to suffer because of my misplaced anger.

The next four years, and after my re-election in 2001, eight years of being in office in Parsippany saw a lot of accomplishments too numerous to mention. Some of the proudest achievements were parks and playgrounds and things related to recreation; support for the emergency services (police, fire, ems, oem, rescue & recovery); new Police Department/Court building, new main Library (of which I had been the Council liaison, shocker), keeping taxes in the bottom 1/3 of the county; and scores of others.

In 2005 I ran for re-election and lost and although my family and friends were devastated, thinking my re-election was fairly certain, I was grateful for the opportunity to serve and knew that when one door closed, another would open. I assumed there was more for me and with my newfound experience and the adage *you win some, you lose some,* didn't make me want to board the Pity Express too eagerly. There was no recount and it was time to keep life moving forward.

I had seen and been through a lot during my political tenure in Parsippany, both personally and professionally. I had gotten married, and later divorced, been on top of the mountain of ego greatness, and been summarily pushed off and treated as insignificant. Nothing is quite as humbling as raising thousands of dollars for yourself at fundraisers where you are the center of attention for hours, and then losing an election and title, and people acting like "who are you again?" Losing was an interesting lesson that brought me back to gaining and losing weight in high school. When I lost the weight, people fawned over me and accepted me as normal. When I lost my election, people treated me as irrelevant. I wasn't sure if losing ever made me a winner.

Hard to please people, isn't it?

With all of my political ups and downs I was also going through career stops and starts.

Zigging and zagging around without much purpose or success, I finally got into local government management full-time in Randolph, NJ after my defeat for a third-term in Parsippany politics and put my management skills to good use. But to understand how I finally landed correctly, we first need to go back in time to see how that winding road started.

Chapter 6

My Life on the

Hamster Wheel

The political journey in Parsippany was quite a wild ride; from nothing to greatness, from being unknown to becoming a household name, to winning and losing elections. While all that was going on, however, there were actual jobs I had in order to pay bills and have a real income. Too many people, myself included on that long list, spent all their time focusing on politics, campaigns, etc., while letting their careers flounder. I was certainly #1 on that list (with a bullet like some used to say about *Billboard 100* singles) for way too many years.

Initially, when I graduated from Seton Hall with my MPA degree, I found a position in the private sector for all of, oh, I would say, three seconds. Well, actually a week, but it was a terrible experience. I thought I was Mr. Bigshot (shocker) having a cool ID employee badge, wearing the corporate casual attire yearned for by so many in my age bracket, and working close to home at a pharma distribution facility.

The images of working with such a short commute, going home for lunch (yay food), and making 'bank' was a thrill. But, as we know, thrills come and go, and after a week of a thoroughly miserable existence, I quit.

I could not quiet the self-actualizing voice in my head telling me fulfillment would not come from serving my bank account; it would come from serving others. Fortunately, I kept feelers out in the real world through the Seton Hall MPA program and came to learn about a job at an affluent private school in Short Hills, NJ as a Development (Fundraising) Associate. I worked with one another person in our office and facilitated fundraising endeavors, public relations and marketing materials, so the position was an extension of my natural talents while teaching me new skills in the fundraising space. Since the political life was taking off at the exact same time, my instinctual and newly acquired interpersonal skills became interchangeable between my full and part-time worlds and the nexus was very beneficial. I helped with the annual fund, newsletter, and even developed their first website; all skills which would repeat throughout other endeavors. I was there from 1996-1998 until I was able to secure what was then, at the time, my "dream job."

I admit my true knowledge of what constituted a "dream job" was somewhat (extremely) limited back then, but at least I had ambition, sort of.

As much as it was great to become a part-time elected official, the goal of working full-time in a government capacity was still prevalent in my thoughts, so when the opportunity to work in county government arrived in a public affairs and information role in the sheriff's office, I was eager to get onboard. Not only was this a coveted political position at the time, it was also the perfect way to have political access and connections 24/7. Was I dreaming? It was not a hard decision to make.

The county sheriff at the time (Ed Rochford) was someone whose campaign had been one of the ones I worked on while living at home and commuting to Rutgers-New Brunswick. He was someone I looked up to, so the opportunity to work with him, and for him, was an honor. It exposed me to operations, budgeting, planning, labor relations and contract negotiations, etc. I was, once again, not too far from home in terms of commute, and the people were great. I was able to attend many political and community-based events with or on behalf of my boss and it expanded my political and social network exponentially.

The money was good (but not great) and there was a cool nexus between full-time government work and part-time elected official duties, or so I thought. Picture Bruce Wayne and Batman and you get the idea.

In hindsight, all the 2 government worlds did was create more of an ego-centric monster who needed more and more adulation and attention from people to satiate the wounded inner child.

Fun and games aside, I learned more about the world and the role government leaders play than I could have in any other position imaginable during the best and worst of times. I worked in this capacity during 9-11, which was surely an eye opener about how law enforcement agencies, and all public safety personnel, stuck together when times get really rough and supported people in need. Although I was not directly involved in any sort of rescue and recovery operations, I was surrounded by people who were, and it made me rethink my role in society and politics.

Finding myself in the midst of widespread tragedy, seeing and speaking with families who had been directly impacted, was jarring to say the least.

I am sure I was not the only one affected in some deeper emotional fashion due the events of those darkest of hours in our nation's history. I saw most in mourning, pain and anger, but there was also inspiration to be found in multiple displays of courage and heroism in the days, weeks and months that followed.

It was only natural that men and women all over the nation, me 100% included, felt the powerful pull not just to aid, but fight as well. While many did find the courage to join the fight that ensued, my battle, along with all elected officials in the nation, required dedication to those who could not fight. It was a frustrating reality for me at first. I wanted to do so much more. With my leadership capabilities, and ability to stay calm under pressure, I considered joining the military but came to the sad, limiting reality that I did not have the courage to make the ultimate sacrifice for my country.

I also received media relations training in Colorado during my time at the sheriff's office. The Columbine shooting was fresh in everyone's mind and the ability to learn from professionals in the field about how to manage the press during terrible circumstances was an education beyond my wildest dreams.

With the support of the sheriff, I was also fortunate to obtain my Certified Public Manager (CPM) professional certification during this time. The CPM program exposed me to an even deeper and more practical level of understanding about how to operate and facilitate good NJ government.

While some aspects of the Seton Hall MPA program were academic or theoretical, everything about the CPM program was spot-on in terms of relevancy to the hands-on, day-to-day operations of municipal, county and state government in the Garden State.

The experience at this position lasted from 1998-2002, or until I decided I needed to make more money and the full-time/part-time government balancing act was not working as successfully as I thought. My ambition had gotten lost somewhere between schmoozing and my desire to live the life of a political Rockstar. In addition to my day job, between meetings, parties, events, classes and the like, I was out 6 or 7 nights a week and I was burned out.

Instead of following my gut instinct and staying in the government/nonprofit space, however, I decided to...you guessed it...go back into the private sector! Awesome!

I decided since other close family members and friends were making better money in the private sector, it was time for me to expand my annual salary, benefits, and be eligible for large corporate bonuses, too!

Dumb. Deja-dumb.

In 2002 and for one approximate year, I worked for an overseas-based pharmaceuticals company located in West Orange, and eventually, Roseland, NJ. I was a senior editor, communications, and worked on things like newsletters, websites, product marketing, etc. I stayed in my expertise and comfort zones and may have changed the end result of what I was selling or pushing to the masses, but the work was very similar to that from the county sheriff and private school, and campaigns, too. I was back into the corporate casual attire and felt important while I mixed and mingled with business executives whose offices were near my office in West Orange (even had a door!). Being back around the Oranges gave me all the comforts Seton Hall had offered – a small professional pond I hoped would encompass the new real-life perspective I thought I wanted after the years of full-time politics. When the company moved its base to Roseland, the now reoccurring realization that I felt empty, unhappy and unfulfilled smacked me square in the middle of the forehead.

As much as I respected the private sector and understood the importance of sales and profits, my hamster cage-like cubicle in Roseland left far too much to be desired.

The best part of my cubicle was definitely the 8x10 photos of President George W. Bush and Vice President Dick Cheney. I'm not sure if they qualified as family, but hey, it filled up what small space I had in my dismal corporate pod.

I was hoping my skill-set was able to be monetized faster and better in the private sector – it was not. I only lasted a year as I couldn't help but feel isolated and lost in that well-appointed but completely miserable corporate building that housed me, Thomas the Hamster, and all of my hamster buddies on their respective wheels, in the middle of nowhere. Being nowhere made me feel like a nobody, like I was back in the endless sea of Rutgers students, floundering for a niche I could fit into. I was one fish in a barrel the size of the Atlantic Ocean. I remember sitting in that cubicle trying to find the nearest window (not close) and would say to myself that life was happening outside of these corporate walls and windows and I was stuck in a 4x4 pseudo-room with partitioned-walls.

The actual work product I delivered was above-average but my mental and emotional health was suffering in the process. I did achieve the desired corporate bonus and bought myself a very shiny (gently used) famous two-tone Swiss watch that I had coveted since I was a kid. Now I was really important...or so I thought.

More on the watch later...

My next full-time position in 2003 was working for a stand-alone community-based hospital in Pequannock, NJ. It was the hospital I was born at, *along with Derek Jeter,* and it was a really cool idea to go back to where it all began. I worked in the Foundation office and performed, you guessed it, fundraising! I worked with a great staff who partnered together to coordinate grants, annual giving, events such as a Golf outing, Gala, Wine Tasting and Race. I wrote and edited content for press releases and brochures and coordinated the phone/mail annual giving campaign. Working at a small hospital was like being back at Seton Hall (thank God!) – small campus-like setting with really nice people who were working together for the betterment of the customers.

Helping people was always a passion of mine, it was the original reason I got into politics, so helping raise money for a hospital organization I deeply cared about, so they could invest in technology and equipment to help improve and save lives, was fantastic. I was Jerry Lewis once again!

A constant theme of this book is definitely the tug-of-war of service vs. self. It was only when I found Christ in 2015 that the tug-of-war game finally ended with love, peace, hope and joy as the victors and fear, anxiety, despair and regret as the losers.

While this was going on, it was time to plan for the 40th wedding anniversary for my parents at Villa Domenico's Italian Restaurant on Route 46 in Parsippany, NJ in October. As I was working at the hospital, I noticed that my shiny new (old) Swiss watch wasn't making me feel good or important anymore. I would walk around thinking I was all that and a bag of chips, but deathly afraid I was going to scratch, ding or dent the darn thing. There were competing thoughts of greatness and abject fear which permeated my daily existence. *It didn't mean as much to me to have this awesome watch I coveted since I was a little lower-middle class boy from Lincoln Park and Parsippany, I wondered.*

As the calendar turned (and watch ticked) toward the anniversary dinner party I was coordinating with my sister Lisa, I decided to take the watch back to the jeweler and sell it. It didn't make me happy or help my personal life, it just made me a guy with an overpriced Swiss watch that actually didn't tell accurate time. I was too paranoid to wear it or damage it. I no longer needed physical proof that I had grown from my personal and financial status as a child. It was impressive, but not really me. I took the money and put it towards the majority of the cost of the anniversary dinner for my parents, and at the event I made sure, during my speech of course, to thank "our sponsor", the famous Swiss watch company. Their 40th was far more timeless.

The experience at the hospital was great for two years until I lost my bid for a third term in Parsippany politics in 2005. Losing the primary in June of that year was painful for everyone around me (their egos had come to enjoy a certain way of life and level of attention), but not me. I was relieved to be done with my tenure and to re-focus on my full-time career life. While I was happy at the hospital, there was no opportunity for solid advancement, and I was stuck. I looked into parlaying all of my (varied but eerily similar) experiences into a better paid full-time position in government. It was time to put politics aside and get real.

As I was looking to move into another position, I experienced a very unusual day at the office. On a random July day, I received a phone call out of the blue from a person requesting information about donations…specifically of organs. It sounded legitimate so I gave details about same but as the call went on, I realized the caller was planning to commit suicide. A real-life bat signal lit before my very eyes. I remained calm and kept the caller on the phone while contacting the hospital's social services and crisis intervention personnel. I knew I had to take the caller seriously. I heard the sadness, despair and uncertainty in the man's voice, and I knew I had to keep him on the phone as long as possible until we could get help to him. I obtained pertinent information from the caller and at the same time searched the Internet for additional information on him. I continued the conversation until help arrived at the caller's door. I was told later that my actions went well beyond the normal workday for a non-clinical person, but I just treated it as simply helping a fellow human being in need. I was finally a superhero to someone who desperately needed one and my inner Batman smiled in approval. It was like a sign I was looking for, that it was ok to move my life on.

I was nominated by three people at the hospital for the September employee Service Star Award. Each month the hospital honored one employee whose performance exceeded expectations and set him or her apart as a role model for others. I was formally recognized at a ceremony in the hospital by the hospital president attended by many fellow employees. My parents and former boss, the county sheriff, also attended. I even had a celestial star named after me. During a clear night, if you look up into the sky, you will see Big Dipper, Little Dipper, and me, Ego-Major. I guess if you are going to go big, you might as well go intergalactic. "Tom was exceptional in his ability to handle such a situation and deserved recognition by his peers," said Clara Vogt, Assistant to the Director of Materials Management at the time, who was one of three people who nominated me for the coveted Service Star Award. "Tom's quick thinking and calmness helped save a life."

As life should have it, the stars really did align with me in mind and the opportunity to be assistant township manager in the affluent suburban Morris County community of Randolph, NJ opened up while I was being recognized at the hospital and having an internal debate about future career endeavors.

I interviewed successfully for this coveted position (there are not many assistant manager or administrator positions in the state of NJ) and started soon after the awards ceremony in the later part of 2005.

There are certain professional experiences we have in life that could be considered game-changers. Positions that propel us to the next level of challenge, authority, responsibility, and compensation. Thus far I have detailed a variety that might fall into this category for me. The position described next would be first and foremost on this list.

What exactly does an assistant township manager do, I wondered? Well, obviously whatever the boss tells you to do, but more specific than that, I learned how to appropriately operate a government agency on a day-to-day basis, not from the dais, but from the back offices, with research, thoughtful planning, lots of paperwork and collaboration.

I thought as an elected official I knew all I needed to about how to run government, managing people and budgets. How naïve. The real work was not done by the elected officials who showed up 2x a month for a few hours to set policies, as important as that function was.

The real work was done by dozens and hundreds (or thousands in larger communities) of dedicated public servants who worked full or part-time, or volunteered, in a variety of positions and titles to make government effective and efficient, and responsive to the taxpayers. It was truly an amazing display of collaboration from individuals who clearly upheld many of the same values and ideals I did – helping, serving, being a part of something greater. These were my kind of people and my boss was one terrific mentor!

I managed the operations of a purchasing cooperative where we were the lead agency for over 200 paid government members. I was responsible for the creation and dissemination of the six-year capital budget. I participated in negotiations with all employee bargaining units. I worked with department heads on the timely distribution of monthly statistical reports for Council members. I managed the IT and telephone system infrastructure.

I served as liaison to the Open Space Committee and negotiated with outside agencies for purposes of open space acquisition. I managed the creation of the eight-page quarterly Township newsletter (once again) and yearly annual report/calendar.

83

I maintained and updated the Township website (once again) and performed all duties as acting township manager when required.

Not only did I enjoy the work, but I was able to, similar to my experience at the county sheriff's office, learn from someone who was truly well-respected in the industry. The township manager, John Lovell, was a legend in the field and prided himself on mentoring the next generation of government leaders which in itself spoke to the strength of character he possessed and one others (myself included) should hope to one day aspire to.

His gift of leadership, apparent the moment he walked into any room, political or otherwise, did not exist in selfish or power-driven motives. It existed in the form of wisdom and the passing of knowledge from one generation to the next for the betterment of everyone near him. I was thankful to experience all he had to offer. Learning from him was like combining the Seton Hall MPA degree and the Certified Public Manager program all in one.

Were there a Mount Rushmore of my industry, he would deservingly be placed front and center as a visionary in the realm of local government.

The knowledge base I absorbed from him and many others in Randolph during those crucial years set me up for the next chapter of life (and this book!).

When interviewing John for this book (Winter 2018/2019, he said:

"Capable Town Managers learn to balance the needs of a demanding public and elected officials, assessing information received from staff and various agencies. Decisions are made; problems are solved; and momentum is achieved. Tom Russo has proven to be a capable manager as he has an innate ability to assess information and communicate informed decisions. From the beginning of Tom's time in Randolph, I felt comfortable relying upon his counsel and solid perspective."

I was there for four great years until I was finally able to move into the big chair. Front row here I come! But once again, the political ego demons resurrected and almost derailed everything. Swimming in the cesspool once again was going to leave quite a smell.

It will be later in my story where I understood the nexus between doing good and being relevant was faith. You can do good…but if it is only in the service of yourself and not others, it doesn't work. You can be relevant…but if you achieve status or recognition in this world for all the wrong, immoral reasons, it doesn't work. Faith becomes the bridge between doing good for others and being relevant in God's eyes since we are perfectly created by Him. Doing good and being relevant are not mutually exclusive.

Chapter 7

Politics Redux:

The Ego Strikes Back

I remember the day I got the phone call. It was from the recruiter hired by the small northwest NJ town of Newton, NJ. He knew me from mutual social circles in our municipal government industry and was always very kind to me. As we went through our light banter, he asked me a very intriguing question – "what did I think about applying" for this town manager position he was looking to fill in this sleepy little county seat town?

I have to admit. When he asked me the question, I just stared at my computer screen and said to myself, "where is that"?

After four successful years of work in that affluent suburban Morris County town, I wasn't sure I was ready to move on and go to some remote location where I would need my passport to enter and leave the county.

But, as the inner demons debated the pros and cons back and forth like my old college debating days, I said I was interested and let him make his obligatory consultant's sales pitch.

While he was going through the joys of being a town manager in Newton, I was quickly researching the town on the Internet. I first went to the town's website and noted the retro-look and feel (and I don't mean that in a complimentary fashion).

Ugh. *I am going back in time, I thought. Well, this isn't going well. This is a step backwards, right?* But after I pushed the ego aside, I delved into some interesting articles in various newspapers and publications about "redevelopment" and "vision plan" and "outside consultants" who were being used to chart a different course for the little hamlet. I told the recruiter that I would give it a shot and send in my materials.

I went into Tom-mode and did my usual excessive amount of interview preparation and diligence. I visited the town during some vacation time and drove all the streets, residential and commercial areas.

I noted the very Norman Rockwell-esque look of the downtown, with trees, and nice retail signage, and walkability, and a variety of small shops and eateries. Hmm, I thought, this town had "great bones" as we say in the local government vernacular.

Boy, with some improvements here and there, this place could be a northwest Morristown, Red Bank, Westfield, or Hoboken. On a smaller scale, mind you, but definitely could trend in those respected and respectable directions.

I went to the municipal building to get a street map and ask what the best place in town was for lunch. The purpose of the map was twofold: it was to have a practical guide for my Amerigo Vespucci-like excursion; but it was also to test the staff to see how they treated random customers from remote Hoth-like planets like Parsippany.

When I asked the town manager's assistant for a lunch spot recommendation and she told me the national chain restaurant on the state highway, I was like, no, I meant local place where locals go, and she advised of a bar/grill type joint on the main street of the bucolic downtown. I thanked her for both suggestions and continued forward.

At the bar/grill I did what any person does when they want dirt (I mean information) on the locale – I asked the bartender.

He was very kind and tolerated my 20-questions on the downtown, community as a whole, and the interesting things going on with redevelopment. I was impressed with his level of institutional knowledge and the food wasn't bad either. My full brain and belly were most pleased, and we moved on.

Later, I would visit Newton on a Saturday, when hundreds of residents would be at the local theatre to hear about a new planning vision for the town. It was very interesting and great to see the locals care about Newton's future.

When I went through the several round of interviews, the aforementioned recruiter was very kind in his observations of my preparation, as evidence of same must have been fairly prevalent during the extensive grilling sessions. He told me I should teach a class on interview prep, and I took that, coming from someone of his expertise in the field, as a very high compliment, indeed.

I was able to secure the position after several rounds of offers and contract negotiations and started in August of 2008.

For many years, this town would be my career-life, spending countless hours, days and nights, working with staff and volunteers and professionals on improving a town that had seen better days earlier in its history when it was more of an industrial and manufacturing center like many other NJ towns.

But as the years turned, we saw major improvements in businesses and industry coming (and going, too), social media and marketing, our police/fire/ems/oem, parks and recreation, town finances, overall customer service, and even the school system (managed by a separate board of education) making major strides towards improved scores and reputation. Though by no means easy or simple, the responsibility of managing a small town, one with 8,000 residents, 3.1 square miles, a hospital, a community college, county government, and over 300 businesses, was a daily thrill and challenge. Although it should have been enough for me, it wasn't.

During my years at this position, I got remarried to a wonderful woman with two daughters. Our blended family formerly began in the summer of 2012 and we purchased a lovely one-acre home and property in Bernards, NJ, in the tony Basking Ridge section of town.

One of the first things I did, when I should have been unpacking moving boxes of useless things I would never use again, I applied to be a volunteer with the town as a member of the Library Board of Trustees. Since I had been the liaison in Parsippany to its wonderful library system and spent most of my life in a library somewhere (you did read the previous chapters, right?), the thought process was sound. I was accepted into the fold and started my endeavor in the beginning of 2013.

I was eager to participate in discussions as this library was engaged in a debate about its future and renovations and expansion. Right up my alley, I thought, as we did the same thing in Parsippany when we were looking to improve its multiple library system. As the year progressed, I was happy with my full-time endeavors in Newton and my volunteer efforts in Bernards.

And then…the ego struck back. It was subtle at first, and then all-consuming in the end.

I decided to get back into politics, in purely a volunteer capacity mind you, in a local campaign. I enjoyed dusting off my Karl Rovian-like abilities to be involved and engaged in campaign activities. What could be the harm, right? Unfortunately, what it did was open the portal back to the wounded inner child who strived for inappropriate adulation, attention, and the incessant need to be liked and admired.

The powers that be in town liked my work and background, and at one point asked me if I would be interested in being appointed to the Zoning Board of Adjustment for 2014. Since that was another comfort zone from my previous life in Parsippany, my redemption tour continued, and I said yes. My future was bright. But inside I was dim.

The sages of Basking Ridge also asked me about running for a township committee position. At first, I laughed and scoffed at the suggestion as it would be like going backwards in time after I had just spent a decade moving my life and career and finances way forward.

Instead of listening to my gut instincts, which were screaming to stay away from the dark side, I kept inching closer and closer to it. I was moving away from things that were important to me like my family and career, into the dark world of politics I thought I had been done with and had been done with me. It was like a moth to a flame, or a bug to a bug zapper, and I was in the political tractor-beam of hell.

It was strange. One night, I went to bed, confident in my decision not to run for any office again and get involved in the cesspool that I knew was politics. And when I woke up the next morning, it was like something overcame me in my slumber, and I was hell-bent on world-domination, or at least electoral redemption at the local government level.

I didn't listen to those rationale inner voices (which I would later learn to be the Holy Spirit, post-September 2015), I did what many reformed addicts do, I fell off the wagon…and ran for office.

I did my usual levels of research, outreach, and due diligence, and was successful in securing a position during the County Committee screening process in March on a two-person ticket. The primary and general elections were not really very interesting or close and I was victorious.

Actually, I filled an unexpired term in October of that year and started my own full term in January of 2015. And so, my three-year stint back in political life began. Yippee.

Right now, there is someone reading this saying to themselves, Tom, that was great! You got elected to a new political position in a different NJ town, you were good at politics, had a great background, and could contribute great ideas and things. You were the phoenix again and rose from the political ashes to greatness! And my answer to that would be – *all that glitters is not gold. Re-read the Swiss watch story from Chapter 6 and you will know what I mean. "Watch" what you wish for, you just might get it.*

I spent most of my time dreading the meetings and obligations. They took me away from the work I truly enjoyed, and was meant to be doing, in Newton. And they pushed me away from my family, friends, and other more meaningful social and volunteer activities.

It was like being on a train that you know is going to wreck and you can't stop it. Ever have that feeling? Like you want to be in control of circumstances and situations, but because your head is so far up your rear-end you can't tell forwards from backwards?

Well, that was me. Good ol' political Tom.

I let the title and ego get the best of me. I made bad decisions in all aspects of my life. Personally, professionally, and financially, I was drowning in all facets.

I was depressed and spent a lot of time alone, crying about my life and where it had gone. It was all my fault, mind you, but when you are that low you really don't spend too much time using a Gantt chart to determine the appropriate place and time for fault or blame.

I was miserable...and it was torture. But it wasn't just torture for me as I was not the husband I should have been nor the stepfather my girls needed. I looked at people in Newton differently because now I was elected Mr. Bigshot in my affluent hometown and the humble, simple people in Newton were treated by me as less-thans instead of as the decent human beings they were.

I grin-f***ed everybody and spent less time with my family all around, and I minimized time with friends who had been loyal and with me for many years.

The walls continued to move in on me, getting closer and closer to the point where I could no longer breathe nor look at myself in the mirror. It wasn't like years past when I couldn't do that because I didn't want to look at the Fat Tom. It was worse. I didn't like myself anymore as a human being and could not tolerate the hypocrite I became. I wasn't perfect like I pretended to be, far from it. I didn't respect my marriage, my kids or my simple life. I took for granted everything God gave me because my wounded inner child needed more…craved more…attention, adulation. Always seeking approval from the outside instead of from within. Forty years of self-esteem issues will do that to you.

Eventually, everything crashed in on me. I was underneath the emotional rubble I had created, and the world was spinning out of control. I no longer could keep up the charade. The happy, simple life I truly wanted was elusive. The shallow life I was living destroyed my will to live and created a wake of devastation around me. I was done. Finished. This is how it would end. *It needed to end.*

How did I get here? How did I, the strong, egotistical Type "A" Chief Executive, wind up on my hands and knees begging to be saved?

There was nowhere to run anymore.

I couldn't talk my way out of this. I couldn't pretend I was perfect when I wasn't.

After 43 years of a life full of shallowness and vapid behavior, of days and nights where I thought I had all the answers, I finally realized I wasn't even asking the right questions, if I was asking any questions at all. Having all the answers was easy when I was the smartest person in the room. Surrounding myself with those I deemed (unfairly) to be lesser, those who would not have the intellect or worse, the confidence to question me, brought my ego to new heights. And I loved it.

My ego and I could do anything, achieve anything, and make others lose sight of what was most important to them. I was an expert in adaptation, a professional chameleon, a personal charmer, and could move people at will like pawns on a chess board they never knew existed. Their morals and ethics were quickly scattered and lost to the wind, clearly no match for the game I played day in and day out. Success came at all costs and I not only believed but lived my own press releases – I was a genius and could do no wrong.

How ironic it was the same ego that had blinded everyone from the attractive sycophants across the room, to the political arena I conquered, had made me its first willing victim, blind to the fact I had no moral compass, no religious faith to keep me grounded, no unyielding beliefs, no true core. I was just another unsuccessful member of a large church who had more guilt than any real relationship with God. I needed to end this pain, this self-righteous existence I created for myself while I stepped on the emotional toes of everyone around me to get to the top rung of some superficial ladder. "Why God, why am I this way?", I cried out on the floor, alone in my expansive and well-appointed, now utterly useless office. "I don't want to live this lie anymore – I am tired of being a fraud – please help me and I vow to change my ways if you will show me how. I don't have the answers anymore."

It was at that moment a never before experienced sense of calm came through every fiber of my being. It was then I heard a voice say, "Tom…it's time."

There was no one else there with me, except Jesus.

Unless you have been saved, it is hard to describe. I had never been that low in my life, contemplating ending my life as I knew it because it seemed easier and the right thing to do.

I got up off of that floor, dusted myself off, and felt a clarity of purpose. It felt like that moment in my youth when I threw up off of the front steps of my childhood home in Lake Parsippany. When I decided being the fat kid was no longer interesting or fun or tolerable. When I decided to get my butt in gear and lose weight. Except this time, it was not about weight, or image, or superficial ego-boosting activities. No, I had been there and done that. It was about changing my life, from the inside out, instead of from the outside in. I was going to let Jesus into my heart and change things for the better.

The people around me were counting on me to be the best Tom I could be. Not the Political Tom, or the Title-loving Tom, but just a decent, hard-working Christian man who would love faithfully and live an admirable life. It was time to grow up spiritually and emotionally. I knew I needed a different path, and I needed help finding it.

Chapter 8

My Faith Crawl:

Hope <u>and</u> Change

Whew! It's been some roller coaster ride, hasn't it? Madone! Thank you for taking the time to learn about me from the womb going forward! I am truly grateful you made it this far in the book, because I am grateful I made it this far in life.

Now it's time to turn the page and get this faith party started! You have faithfully suffered through the ordeal that was the first part of my life, now we get to kick things into high gear and explore spiritual faith from multiple angles and avenues, and then we are going to talk about some really cool ways you, too, can learn to change your life for you and those around you! I know, that is what you have been waiting for! Me too! Tom is boring! This is a story about how the decisions we make impact those we love, and how we can make things better for everyone if we stay on the righteous path God intended. Amen! Thank you, Jesus!

In fairness, I can't speak to where you are at with your faith. You are going to a church or house of worship and you are really content, or you are jaded about religion or spirituality and trying to find your way. But I certainly can tell you more about my journey of faith, how I found Jesus, and what it means to me to be a born again Christian. My hope is you will see yourself in this journey and open yourself up to change. The future can be bright if you want it to be, so let's get going!

I was raised as a member of a large church as I mentioned earlier in the book, but I really didn't have a close, personal relationship with Jesus. After my step-daughters were confirmed at a local Catholic church, my wife and I made the decision not to go back to the church as we were displeased with the anger and tone displayed by the pastor towards the girls. His attitude contradicted the loving nature of Jesus, so we floundered on our own while our faith dissipated into a black hole of nothingness.

When I hit my darkest hour in September of 2015, I knew I needed something, someone, more powerful and consistent than myself. For me, it was Jesus who turned my life around. I had tried everything else, put myself on the throne, and failed miserably. Why not try something different?

My wife and I began church shopping – which I know some people in the faith community disapprove of, like shopping for a 4K (or now, 8K) television. But we know the pastor and the tone and tenor of the congregation really make a difference in how faithful and consistent you are in your weekly worship.

A pastor friend of mine in Newton recommended Christian Missionary Alliance (CMA) churches that were affiliated with his and we dutifully began our quest for spiritual salvation and excellence. Fortunately for us, Grace Fellowship Chapel in Bedminster, NJ, was one of the first churches we visited, and we hit the jackpot out of the gate! Yazoo! The pastors were both young, dynamic and vibrant, and so was the congregation. I'll never forget how it felt when we pulled our vehicle into a visitor's parking spot that first Sunday, and then departed for the entrance to the church. "Good morning" someone said to us emphatically in the parking lot as we walked along. I was like, "WTF?" Why did these people say hello, who are they, and why are they being pleasant?

In all the years of life I spent in the previous churches, I had never experienced the grace and friendliness of a stranger, certainly not in the parking lot where both vehicles and people tend to be in a rush to enter or leave. Weird, right? I know! But wait, there's more!

When we entered the church, and saw the band, felt the energy, and learned The Word, it was like a breath of fresh air. I couldn't believe my eyes and ears but loved every minute of it.

My hope for you is you find a great Christian house of worship that fills you up inside as much as this one does for me and my wife. **Don't give up.**

However, the weekly church attendance was just the beginning. My wife worked at a local church in the pre-school and the church was hosting a Christian illusionist at an event. It sounded different and interesting and we decided to attend. The event was fun for sure, but that is only half the story.

At the end of the event, the church offered prayer if people were interested, and I went up to one of the friendly gentlemen on the side of the expansive hall and asked for prayer for my life, my marriage, and my family. He dutifully prayed for me and I returned to my seat.

But, then, he came to my seat where I had returned to in tears (I am quite the wus or mushball, depending on your perspective), and advised me of an event with Lonnie Berger, the author of the popular *Every Man a Warrior* (EMAW) book series. I was unfamiliar with Lonnie and the books, but it sounded right up my new faith-filled alley, so I marked the date down.

When the event came soon thereafter, I attended the event solo, with about 100 other men, and some women, and listened as Mr. Berger spoke about how every man is broken and without Christ, nothing will change.

I was mesmerized by both the man and the message, and truly felt God was speaking to me to attend not only this event but the weekly workshops he was speaking about. The EMAW book series is three books which really outline the brokenness of men in all categories (faith, marriage, work, parenting, intimacy, finances, etc.) and how scripture and faith in Christ can be transformative in all regards. I signed up for the classes and much to my surprise, was informed quickly the first class would start up soon. The Thursday night EMAW men's groups, which continue to this day in some form or another, opened my eyes to God's Word and how men are not supposed to have all the answers.

I realized as the series of weekly discussions progressed how much pressure I, and others, had put on me to be perfect, to have all the answers. I realized how much time I wasted in my life focusing on all things and not really consistently succeeding, when I could have been focused on a relationship with God as first and foremost, and how that would open up possibilities and success in all other aspects of my life.

I had the pyramid upside down. Whether it was career, or marriage, or money, or health, or anything, I focused and obsessed, sometimes with great results, and sometimes with great failure. By going through these classes, I learned to really enjoy the quiet moments in life when God speaks to us, to read Scripture to find the answers to life's most perplexing questions, and to recalibrate the people, places, and things I had spent too much time focusing on.

As my faith journey ramped up, and I eliminated certain behaviors, beliefs, activities, and even negative people from my life, I learned of an organization called Pause Ministries located a few miles from me in Basking Ridge, NJ. The mission of Pause was to help men find themselves through a relationship with Jesus Christ. I attended their annual meeting and learned of a 5-day intensive workshop they were hosting for men with multiple speakers and opportunities for prayer and reflection.

I signed up and attended the 5-day intensive in the spring of 2017. It was both the hardest, and best, thing I *ever* did in my life.

Although much of what was said and done there was private and confidential, I can unequivocally tell you the opportunity to be in a safe, loving Christian environment where you can immerse yourself in song and Scripture that is both positive and uplifting; an environment where you can learn from people and professionals who get brokenness and understand the struggles of being a real Christian man in this challenging society, was invaluable. No words can really describe its impact on me.

I came out of that intensive a different man, with a different outlook and different purpose, and I am eternally grateful that I did.

The combination of the weekly church services at Grace and eventual participation in its Mens Group and a baptism ceremony where I publicly declared my newfound faith in Jesus as my Lord and Saviour, coupled with the weekly EMAW program, and the intensive, provided me with a very strong foundation in faith I had never experienced before in my life.

My prayers became frequent and heartfelt, and they were no longer shallow or about Tom. I developed an attitude of gratitude for all the things Christ had given to me, and I began to consistently start each day with Psalm 118:24 – *This is the day the Lord has made, let us rejoice and be glad in it.* It is truly amazing when you start the day with gratitude, how it permeates your being and impacts all of your thoughts and interactions for the day. I highly recommend finding a Proverb or Psalm or some Scripture or uplifting quote that resonates with you and start your day with it, every day – you might be surprised how it sets a different tone and tenor for your daily life.

Finally, I found faith, and hope, in my life. Through the toils and tribulations and darkness, I found the answers to life's questions. But now, it was time to implement the answers and turn everything upside down.

Chapter 9

Progress (Finally)

Now that we have put God back on the throne where He belonged all the time, and removed Tom and his ego, we can look at challenges men face on a daily basis and look at them from a different, healthier perspective.

What I mean by this is – I used to spend time worrying about all aspects of life (health, wealth, family, friends, career, etc.), and found myself not living life to its fullest potential. It was almost, as if, I wasn't taking it to life, life was taking it to me, and I was struggling in all areas. Does that ever happen to you? My focus was completely wrong.

It was only when I found Christ, I truly found inner peace and success and started to focus solely on my relationship with Him.

Let me explain. If you spend all of your time and efforts on the minutia of life, all of the topics, categories and items we men deal with on a day-to-day basis, you get lost in the weeds. Any one success makes you ride higher than a kite; any one failure or step-back might knock you down for days on end.

It makes life a terrible roller coaster ride, and I don't know about you, my stomach can't handle roller coasters!

Instead, by becoming born again, I realized Jesus was my core and foundation, not how my investments were doing today, or how much the scale said I weighed, etc. You change your focus, you change your life! You prioritize things differently. You manage the ebbs and flows of life much better. You have healthier respect for the people and places and things around you. And you have a healthier relationship with yourself.

Hmmm, I can see you are skeptical. Well, let's talk about the 7 key areas of life and chat about how they changed for me. I am pretty confident if you have Christ at your core, you will see changes, too! Wait until you see the next chapter where we talk about the 12 things you give up in the process! Yikes!

One caveat, these are the 7 key areas of life (Lucky 7 as I call them) I focus on, you might have more, or less, but I think this covers most of what we men deal with on a daily basis. And by no means am I a licensed professional in any of these areas. I am just a Christian man trying to find his way through this crazy thing called life.

Please take my observations and opinions as just that, the observations and opinions of a born again Christian who made his life better when he found Jesus.

Lesson 1: Health

As someone who has dealt with the demons of obesity all of my life, I can say this is one of my hardest areas to manage. Before Christ, I was a mess, always obsessing over the scale, how much I ate, grams of carbohydrates, or total calorie count. After I found Jesus, I started to simply focus on the quality of food I ate (organic, low-carb, gluten-free, grass-fed, locally grown produce, etc.), and made sure I ate real food, things that made me feel good inside and provided me with the nutrients and energy I needed to live my life. I went from living to eat, to eating to live. I obsessed less, ate less, moved my body more, and learned to love my body the way God intended.

Lesson 2: Wealth

Another tough topic for Tom! I spent my life overanalyzing budgets (when I had them) in my personal life, always focusing on lack instead of abundance. Ironically, nothing ever really changed for me and I didn't make much traction on money matters this way. Even when my income went up, I still found myself experiencing too much debt and too much worry on a daily basis. What a terrible way to live, right? Obsessing over money doesn't make it work for you. Money is a tool, it is a neutral item that goes where you tell it to go. You need to be intentional about how it is earned and how it is spent, but you don't need to obsess incessantly over it. Furthermore, money is NOT the root of all evil as some people say when they misquote the Bible – the LOVE of money is the root of all evil. You cannot serve God and money. For me, that is an easy one, I choose God every day of the week!

If you find yourself struggling with money, read the Bible, learn its principles, and change your focus. Realize that debt is not a pet! Do not be the borrower who is slave to the lender.

Focus your efforts on something like Dave Ramsey's Debt Snowball or similar program where you get really intentional and hyper-focused on eliminating debt and using your most powerful wealth building tool (income) to save, spend, and give generously. Your life will change, and you will change the lives of those around you.

Lesson 3: Peace and Joy

Ok, who out there doesn't want more of these? Am I right? Life is crazy and hectic and full of ups and downs, sign me up for more peace and joy today!

Seriously, I don't know about you, but on a daily basis I have a million (more or less) things I have to do, take care of, think about, or manage. Especially if you live in New Jersey (Jersey in the house!) like I do, it is a non-stop frenetic pace. Like a race to nowhere.

When I found Christ, I learned how to read the Bible, memorize Scripture, and use quiet time to slow my breathing and thinking down and reconnect with God. Meditation can take a variety of forms. Sometimes I choose to sit in silence outside on my deck or patio and just watch nature. I reflect on how the trees grow in silence.

The birds and the squirrels do their thing and don't worry about social media or the news of the day. Sometimes my meditation might take the form of me listening to jazz music or something else (usually other relaxing music without words) so my mind quiets down and my heartrate normalizes. When some people hear about meditation, they get all weirded out about it or they think it is something hokey. It really isn't.

Same thing for prayer. Before I became born again, I didn't have much of a prayerful relationship with God. Now, I pray before every meal and start my day with Scripture readings and prayers of gratitude for the activities of the day before, and I set intentions for the present day. Sometimes I do it when I am out walking the dog (Lucky!) in the morning so I get the added benefit of the exercise and time with my canine best friend, and nature too. I strongly urge you to make time for God in silence. More often than not, if you are struggling with one or more of these areas I am addressing in this chapter, or those in the next, you will find the answers if you silence your mind and heart and let God in. What do you have to lose?

Lesson 4: Relationships

I don't know about you, but I want my relationships with family members to be inspiring and meaningful. After my relationship with God, nothing is more important to me than my wife and daughters. God has blessed me with them, and I firmly believe I am to live a Godly example for them and take care of them. That is a traditional, old school way of thinking, but it works.

Prior to becoming born again, I was very much focused on my needs and how others could serve me. Not a strong way to live, nor a healthy way to build a loving relationship with your spouse. I also used to bring my work home and treat my daughters like they were staff. Actually, I treated my staff at work better. Not good.

Now, I understand, through Scripture, I am to give up my life and rights for my wife, to love her, protect her, guide her, and strengthen my relationship with God so she can thrive. Finding God has simplified my wants and needs tremendously, and it really helped me understand the feelings and emotions of others rather than my own.

It doesn't mean you lose yourself in the process. Rather, it means with God as your core and foundation, you open up opportunities for loving relationships because you can't give away what you don't have. God is love. Jesus is love. When you have love in your heart, you have love to give.

Lesson 5: Friendships

There are elements of the previous lesson that apply here. Serving others and thinking of the needs of others certainly can apply to your most intimate of family relationships but also to those in your friendship circles as well. Additionally, finding Christ has taught me something even more powerful.

Did you ever read Jon Gordon's book, *The Energy Bus?* If not, I highly recommend it as Jon gives a great illustration about the types of people you will meet in life. Another way to look at life is like a train ride. Some people are meant to get on the train with you early and stay throughout your life. Others get on the train for a stop or two. The thing to keep in mind is this: do not spend or waste time with people that are low energy, or worse, zap the positive energy out of you.

This is not to suggest being mean to people or cruel, not at all. It means we are given a finite amount of time in this lifetime to live. You ever hear the saying "you are only as good as the people you surround yourself with?" Well, it is true. Where you spend your time, and with whom, shows what your priorities are. Choose Godly people and Godly activities. Once you start to compromise in one area, you open yourself up to the enemy and the dark side of life, in all areas. Your friendships should be with people who bring out the best in you. If they do not, it is time to rethink your friendships. Avoid toxic individuals at **all** costs.

Lesson 6: Career

This is a fun one. I definitely have some thoughts to share as, once again, I spent too much of my life obsessing over titles and salaries instead of focusing on what was important. Before I found Jesus, I used to think my title defined who I was. Right? If my business card says I am this, or people around me call me that, then that is who I am. When I found Christ, I realized who I am, and whose I am.

I don't serve people in my positions, I serve God. I don't need a title to be a leader, I am a leader because God made me one. We are all leaders. We are all servants. God gave me unique talents (called spiritual gifts) and I need to honor them by being the best servant leader I can be in any title or role. As my good friend (and the writer of my foreword) Dan Bove told me, "your title is what you do, it is not who you are." Thank God for that!

I also don't worry about job security anymore. Sure, we all want stability in our careers, but that is elusive, now more so than ever. As one of my professors used to say, 'change or die'. The only constant in life is change, so you need to always be honing your existing skills, learning new things, and adapting. You also need to bloom where you are planted. If you always look too far ahead, you won't get there. Whatever your title or position is today, whatever your level in an organization, honor God and do your best. Use your time and talents wisely, and God will reward you.

Finally, when you spend quiet time with God and understand your true purpose, you won't spend as much time worrying about your income level.

When I talk with students at Seton Hall or people mid-career, I give them the following career advice. Think about the things you love to do. The things that you do and don't watch or worry about the clock. Think about where you want to work (geography); the industry; company; then the type of work. People obsess over "I can't make money doing x-y-z" and that is pure bunk. If you are following God's path for your life; if you truly recognize the gifts God has given you; if you are great at what you do; and you apply the principles stated above, I am confident you will attain financial and career success.

Lesson 7: Volunteerism

Before I found Christ, I used to volunteer for many activities and positions, not because I wanted to genuinely help people, but because I needed to feed my ego and build up my political resume. After I found Christ, I realized true volunteerism is an important role for any Christian. We are to serve others, and volunteering for a local organization or nonprofit is a wonderful way to show your love for Christ as you help those less fortunate.

Whatever your cause, whatever your passion, please take time out of your busy day or week to help others. Sometimes we get lost in our own lives and don't realize the suffering of others. Or we say that an hour or two of time won't make a difference for someone else. That is so not true. In fact, if we all did our part and chipped in with our time and talents, many nonprofits would extend their outreach and help many more of our suffering brothers and sisters. Donating our time and talents (and dollars, too) makes a difference. Look within your heart and find a passion for service and go out there and make a difference. You will be glad you did. And, so will God.

Now that we have successfully reviewed the Lucky 7 areas of life that bring us progress…we can delve into the evil twelve. The 12 areas of elimination that finding Christ changed for me, and can change for you, too.

Chapter 10

Process of Elimination

I hope you enjoyed reviewing the Lucky 7 areas of life that change when you seek and find Christ as your Lord and Saviour. Impressive list, right? Now we go into the dark side. These are the character traits or behaviors/beliefs that can be eliminated, or at least recognized and minimized to the greatest extent possible, if you have Christ at your core rather than yourself.

Anger & Resentment

Anger can be a very natural emotion. Seeing a child be abused or bullied, or hearing accounts of genocide throughout the world, can surely make us angry at the perpetrators of these heinous acts. But you cannot fight hate and anger...with more hate and anger. It's not the way of the Lord and it is not the way effective change occurs. Additionally, dealing with pain through anger, and then holding onto resentment, does not yield a great result. Ever experience pain in your marriage, or at work, or with your kids? Surely. The pain of the moment usually leads to anger.

Anger, in the moment, and over time, can lead to resentment. If not dealt with appropriately, the resentment becomes a weapon in today's moments, situations that often have little or nothing to do with the original anger or pain. It is a vicious cycle that goes on and on and on. By activating your innate faith in Christ, you learn how to minimize or eliminate anger. You deal with situations as they come instead of holding onto past transgressions 10, 20 or even 30 years later. You clean the cobwebs out of the attic, if you will accept the analogy, and you clean out the garbage and become pure once again. With meditation, yoga, breathing techniques, quiet time, Scripture and prayer, you can learn to calm the mind and the heart and better handle the toils and tribulations of certain situations without compounding matters with decades old anger and resentment.

Ego

If you have faithfully read the previous chapters and my story, then you know this is one of my favorites! There is nothing quite like a politician with a big ego! Thinking we are at the center of the universe; putting ourselves on the throne instead of God; these are the traits of someone with an ego that is simply too big for primetime.

I am sure you have dealt with this type of individual at work or in your volunteer endeavors; or this describes you. Taking a step back, and acknowledging the awesomeness that is God, really puts your small life in perspective. God is at the center of the universe, not you, and not me. Having a more realistic perspective on this can change how you focus on your life and activities. It makes you realize we are only on this Earth for a finite period of time, and our purpose is to love and serve others, not ourselves.

Control

What goes better (or worse) with ego? That's right! Control. As men we think we need to run everything and be in control of everybody. Sounds great in theory, but it is simply not true. There are very few things in life we can control. What we eat. Where we go. Who we spend time with. So far, so good.

But when we think we can manipulate and control the thoughts, actions, and beliefs of others, that is where we as men go off the rails into the abyss. Do not spend your life trying to control others. We are all created in the image of God.

We are all light beings. We are all spiritual beings having a human experience. However you want to look at, and however you want to describe it, it all comes down to recognizing and accepting our humanity, and controlling our own thoughts and behaviors, and not those of others.

Multi-tasking

I don't know about you, but I am loving this list! It is so painful, yet cathartic, to review the ways of my old life before I accepted Christ. Multi-tasking is a great topic because it describes the fallacy of trying to do too much at one time in the workplace and at home. It sounds great on a resume, and looks good in print, but in reality, it simply does not work. Try making dinner while helping your child with homework, answering work texts, and feeding the dog...while on the exercise bike. Nice try. The insanity of it all would be quite comical if not being so sad. It is not possible for the human mind to focus on more than one thing, effectively, at a time.

If this describes you, stop. Make lists of things to do each day (and yes, even on the weekends). Prioritize them. Know that somedays you might be more productive than others, and that is ok.

While at work you might have twenty key things to do, maybe at home it is less, or more. But if you insist on trying to mentally AND physically focus on more than one task at hand, you are simply setting yourself up for consistent failure. By loving Christ, I simplified my thoughts and actions, and became better able to pace myself, to prioritize things, and to recognize that sometimes it is ok not to be the perfect taskmaster.

Low Self-Esteem

The irony of this one is palpable. Most politicians have HUGE egos…and very, very low self-esteem. It is why they go into politics. They love the adulation and the fame and fortune, because deep down inside, they really don't love themselves, or have not dealt with the inner child wounds of the past. Looking externally for approval never works. Trust me. I tried it for decades. It was only when I accepted Jesus that I realized God already made me whole. I was pure in the womb and right out of the gate. I didn't need the approval or recognition from family, friends or strangers. That sense of peace and purpose was already installed in MY unique database by God.

Recognizing who you are, and whose you are, changes your view about others and yourself. By becoming a part of a good Bible-based church; by reading Scripture; by spending quiet time with the Lord, you will know God has already given you the ultimate Good Housekeeping seal of approval and you don't need it from anything or anyone else.

Perfection

Are you seeing a trend with this list? All these things are really bad for you, or really impossible to manage and deal with. Perfection is an elusive goal. Trying to be perfect in the workplace and solve every problem. Trying to be perfect in a marriage and be the breadwinner and hero. Trying to be superdad and be everything to your kids, all the time. Not possible. The real goal, friends, is to achieve excellence. To recognize the beauty of our imperfections. To work and strive for the best, surely, but to seek excellence in all actions and activities. God has already given us a playbook for life, called the Bible. If you simplify your life and know God has already given you the answers to life's questions, it makes a world of difference. Don't try to be perfect. Be you.

Selfishness & Narcissism

Ooopha. I wonder if this list is as painful for you as it is for me. But sometimes we need a strong dose of reality to persevere, and #7 goes right to the heart of a lot of our problems as men. I, I, me, me. Right? Depending on how we were raised, our birth order, our relationship with others in childhood, we learned our place in life and how we landed in the pecking order. Always focusing on yourself really clouds your judgment on all things. How we treat our wives. How we handle money and finances. How we raise our children. If we always view ourselves as separate beings, then we never really connect or integrate our lives with others. If we follow Jesus and think of service to others, we recalibrate so much of our thinking and efforts. It doesn't mean we neglect ourselves or our basic needs; then we are unable to mentally or physically function and that does not help anyone. Rather, it means we take care of our basic needs, and use our remaining energy to give love and support to our loved ones; to give guidance and mentoring to our work colleagues; and to give a helping hand to nonprofits and those in need through volunteerism. There is a lot of pain and suffering in this world because we focus on ourselves and not the needs of others. Take a step back and thank God for your blessings, your time, and your talents. And push them out into the world. Brother, the world needs you.

Emotional Immaturity

I like sports. I like video games. I like superheroes. I like me some PB&J! Yes, yes, yes and heck yes! However, these are not exactly the life changing things God wants us to focus on. Sure, it is simple fun and can be great outlets for energy release when we are stressed about life, money, marriage, children and work. However, if we stay stuck in the mentality of a child (ooh, I forgot chicken nuggets, too), if we pout when we don't get our way at home of the office, or we expect others to do for us like a parent-child relationship, then we are simply not being Godly men. This might be one of the most painful topics on this list, because unless you have gone to counseling or done an intensive like I did, you might not have taken the time to address inner child (or children) wounds. I recommend speaking with a pastor in your church, finding a good Christian counselor, or even reaching out to my good friend Dan Bove at Pause Mens Ministries in Basking Ridge, NJ (pauseministries.org) if you want to learn how God can heal these wounds and elevate you to the time and place of life you should be in. I must warn you: this can be an extremely raw process and the most painful of demons to exercise, but also from a foundational standpoint, the most important to draw you closer to Christ. Growing up is hard, but necessary, to follow God's plan and purpose for your male adult life.

Insecurity

Until they find Christ, most men will spend their lives worrying about what others think of them. As the great John Wooden once said, "Be more concerned with your character than your reputation because your character is what you really are, while your reputation is merely what others think you are." When you focus on things that are not of God's world, think of this list, you move yourself further and further from source energy. You become less and less of who you were meant to be. If we always worry about the thoughts and opinions of others, we will never have true happiness because people are very finicky. Unless, they too, have found Christ, they can love you one day and hate you the next. They can need you one day and avoid you the next. This is not the roller coaster ride you want to go back on over and over again with an unlimited pass. Do not focus on what other human beings think of you. Focus your attention on the fact that God made you in His image, that He sent His only begotten son, Jesus Christ, here to die on the wooden cross in a very painful death to forgive your sins. And that He placed the Holy Spirit inside of you as your moral compass to guide you through the ups and downs of life. Find your security in knowing the only Father that won't let you down, The Lord our God. Be secure in knowing who loved you first and who will love you the longest.

Lack of Communication Assertiveness

Just like in baseball, once in a while you have to throw a curveball to get the hitter off his game. This one is meant to do that for you. Not something you might typically find in a Christian self-help book, it is an area that most men really don't deal with until they have a problem in a relationship. I am going to address it head-on because I think it is a component of helping you become a more well-rounded Christian man in all aspects of your life. Repeat after me: I feel. Whoa. Are you ok? Did you fall off your chair? Trust me, when I learned how to do this it certainly felt like a bicycle without training wheels. Men are not taught, especially in our society here in the U.S., to acknowledge our feelings, and better yet, to express them verbally to others. When you have found your comfort and salvation in the Lord, you change how you handle situations. When you develop this sense of peace and inner strength through Jesus, it changes how not only you connect with others, but how you indeed connect with yourself. By recalibrating the system that is you, you are able to (1) gain understanding and truth about your needs and wants; and (2) safely and reasonably articulate them to others without fear of reprisal or conflict. If you are thinking and acting in a Godly way to yourself and to others, then the fear of rejection from others goes away. You are comfortable in your own skin.

And you can talk about feelings with others and not worry about their opinions or reactions because you are appropriately articulating what God has placed inside of you. Coming from a safe place and being able to talk about life is a huge positive for men when they develop a loving relationship with Jesus. Try it. You will be glad you did. And so will others around you, too.

Fear

A precursor to Chapter 12 of this book (sorry, you still have to read on, you can't stop here you are doing great my brother from another mother!), fear is the thing that holds us back from most success in life. Friends, in every situation, there are only two choices: fear or love. Choose love. God is love. That simple. We will go into more details later...hold the thought (index finger in the air).

Keeping Up with The Jones'

Ah, the Jones'! I think they live across the street from me. Actually, I have no idea who lives across the street from me. My point is this. If we do not seek a loving relationship with God and are not comfortable in our own skin and have an attitude of gratitude for what we have, we spend our lives looking outside ourselves for happiness and approval.

There is no worse example of this than trying to keep up financially with others. Oh, look at their house, I wish I had that. Wow look at Johnny's new truck, that is awesome, I wish I had that. I wish my spouse was like so-and-so. And on, and on, and on. The Jones' are broke and stupid and unfulfilled. They have a mortgage that could choke a horse (sorry Mr. Ed), Sally Mae lives in their spare bedroom, they are getting fleeced on their car leases, and the shiny two-tone Swiss watches they wear don't even tell time as accurately as yours does with the Japanese quartz movement. Ouch. I know, talking about money and marriage is taboo and a punch to the gut, but I am Tyson baby and I am going in for the TKO in Round #12 here! *Do not spend your life trying to be like someone else.* Do not try to keep up financially with others because you THINK they are doing better than you. Run your own race. Stay in your own lane. Follow Biblical principles on life, love, money and marriage. Don't be someone other than the Godly person He made you to be.

A lot of meat on the bones in this chapter, right? (Ribeye!) I hope you have enjoyed, or at least appreciated, the direct thoughts and opinions shared on the evil twelve. I know it was painful to write for me, but I expect the twelve might have been just as painful for you to read.

We are in this together my brothers in Christ! Together we can do all things with Him. *You are not alone in this battle.* Let's strap the armor on and keep fighting our way through this into Chapter 11. Now that we have made progress in Chapter 9 and eliminated certain beliefs and behaviors in this current chapter, we can learn how to go through ANY brick wall the enemy puts in our way of a loving, close relationship with Christ. Let's rock!

Chapter 11

Overcoming Obstacles

It is not the goal in life to perfectly avoid obstacles or pretend they do not occur. Rather, it is to acknowledge we are imperfect beings in a broken (imperfect) world, surrounded by broken (imperfect) people. Our goal, then, is to recognize such and to work towards resiliency and perseverance. The challenges will come, often times when you least expect them (no one effectively plans for the death of a friend or loved one, the loss of a job, pain in a marriage or relationship, etc.). Brothers, it is ok to find yourself on the pity pot once in a while, but not for too long, for your legs will get numb and tired and how then will you effectively move forward and get moving? My rule of thumb is 24-hours; everyone is allowed a full day to remember, reflect, mourn, feel pain, and move on. Granted, this number is completely arbitrary and can and should vary based on experience, personality, and circumstance. The point of this is to recognize life is a precious gift and tomorrow is never guaranteed – we are meant to live life to its fullest extent possible on a daily basis, and not obsess over things in the rearview mirror (the past).

Our eyes are meant to be looking forward through the expansive windshield of life (the future). Think of a car – the rearview mirror is always smaller than the windshield and for good reason.

Life is the same. God wants us to be faithful and forward-thinking. Being in a perpetual state of denial or mourning is not what God intended for us. We need to feel the pain, we need to walk towards the pain, feel it, live it, and let it go. Let's talk about five (5) key specific points here:

♦ Men are Overwhelmed/Running on Empty
♦ Marital Stress/Financial Stress/Issues with Children are Real
♦ Obstacles can be Your Own Inner Dialogue, Others, Lack of Support
♦ Own Your Mistakes
♦ How Obstacles Impact Those Around You

Let's be honest. As men we are all trying to do too many things at too many times, and we don't always succeed. The Superman syndrome. We want to be great at home, for our spouse and children, and then go to work and be respected and admired and rock it out there.

Sounds great, right? Well, doesn't always work out that way if we don't take time to recognize our humanity and acknowledge God as the source of energy, wisdom, and life.

Multitasking and trying to do too many things do not make you successful, they make you tired and overwhelmed and ineffective. *Running on Empty* may be a great Jackson Browne song, but running on empty in life is no fun. Harness your limited energy on specific tasks on a daily basis at home and work; don't try to do too much; aim for quality of work not quantity and you will see different results.

The second key point is marital stress, financial stress, and issues with children are all a part of life. Fairy tales are not real. Money issues happen. Children will not always be perfect and loving. Get it? We are brought up to think that effort will guarantee awesomeness in all these areas and we spend our time and energy on same. Those efforts can be harnessed differently, and we will talk about that later.

The third point is obstacles come in various shapes and sizes. They can be the inner voice inside of you telling you can't do or accomplish something. They can be the family member or friend or colleague today who tells you achieving this or that is impossible or improbable.

They can also be the lack of support you receive in a particular endeavor or project. Obstacles will always come, it is how you deal with them that matters.

The fourth point to recognize is to own your mistakes! This is a tough one for many men as we like to blame others, our parents, our childhood, our co-workers, our spouses, Democrats/Republicans, etc., for a particular problem or circumstance. Sorry Charlie, but you need to own up to where you are at in life and what you did to make your circumstances a reality. If struggling to own your mistakes describes you, don't get too down on this one, the advice is coming to help you work through this.

The last point is recognizing how obstacles impact those around you. The same challenges and issues you are dealing with can and most probably are ones your family and friends and co-workers are dealing with, too. You are not in this alone. Men tend to isolate and ruminate more than they should rather than seeking support and advice from others. Thinking you have all the answers, all the time, doesn't work.

I know what you are thinking. Tom just laid out a great list of key points, a reality check, but now what? Aha! I knew it.

No faith! Not only do I have actionable steps to overcome obstacles for you my friend, I have some Bible verses to reinforce them. Nice!

Hitting the "Pause" Button on Life.

As my good friend Dan Bove, president of Pause Ministries, will attest to, men are always going fast and hard on all activities, and sometimes, we just need to hit the "Pause" button on life. What does that mean? It means exactly what it says. When you are going 100 miles an hour in your marriage, in your career, with your kids, etc., and nothing seems to be going well, you need to BREATHE...

RELAX...

REFLECT...and find comfort in God.

I know before I became a born again Christian, I thought I had to be all things to all people, and just keep going and going. Some of that was self-inflicted as I always felt I needed to be a high-achiever. As Dan says, men need to go from 'chaos to calm' by hitting the "Pause" button and take the time to reflect on God and life. How often do you consider all aspects of your life including faith, family, work and relationships? If you are always going fast and furious, you are missing out on a lot of the little intricacies that make life really special.

Recognize the Obstacles Within.

Have you ever heard of a SWOT analysis? It is a very useful tool in business I will describe and refine for your individual utilization. SWOT stands for Strengths-Weaknesses-Opportunities-Threats. When I do this activity in my current work as town manager, I usually spend a ½ day with key thought leaders in the organization, at various titles, levels and positions, and delve into the deep nuances of the organization. I will give you a quick business example and then I will help you create your own SWOT.

A strength for a business could be its unique product line. Let's say it makes widgets that are highly-specialized and unique in the marketplace. A weakness might be the cost to make widgets is too high. An opportunity, then, might be to move the production of the widgets to a different location or country to cut production costs. A threat might be a lack of a trained workforce to work on the widgets in other locations.

Make sense? Now let's apply this tried and true business practice to YOUR life.

Take a sheet of yellow legal pad paper, turn it from portrait to landscape, and write SWOT at the top. Create 4 equally sized columns underneath, and label them S, W, O and T. Now think about your personal strengths. I am not looking for arrogance here, I am looking for brutal honesty about you, your life, your passion, your strengths and opportunities for growth. The more honest you are in assessing yourself, the greater the opportunity for change and success.

Some examples of strengths might be related to soft skills like humility, empathy, listening skills, communication skills, etc. They might also relate to things like technical knowledge, education, experience, etc.

Now, think about your weaknesses. Tough right? Think about how you perceive yourself, but also take the time to reflect about how others might describe you. Even if you think others might not always understand you or know you, I bet you can think of a few family members or co-workers who can read you pretty well. Weaknesses could be short temper, anger, arrogance, lack of sympathy, lack of technical skills, lack of education, unwillingness to change, etc.

Take a few moments now to look at your strength and weaknesses. Are they honest and true? Until you can say yes, do not leave this point in the exercise. Please keep in mind these lists can and should relate to you professionally AND personally. What are your strengths at work? Are they the same or different than those in your marriage or with your kids? I know many men who are very patient with their subordinates at work but then lose that patience when they are home with their wife and kids, or vice versa. Note any incongruence between your work life and personal life and be honest about it.

When you are ready, look at the weaknesses, what kind of opportunities do they present? A weakness is not something to be embarrassed about, nor are they what I would consider to be fatal flaws. They are opportunities for growth and change. Write down the opportunities that each weakness presents.

Finally, what are the threats to your opportunities for growth and change? Money or lack thereof? Time? Willingness to change? Lack of knowledge or technical skills? Negative people in your life that you might need to distance yourself from? Old childhood thoughts that prevent you from living your best life?

Threats can come in all shapes and sizes, but recognizing they exist is one of the first key steps to overcoming life's challenges.

I am confident if you are honest with yourself, and you put the time and effort into this important exercise, you will have a living, breathing document that can assist in improving your life.

Prayer and Meditation.

Now that you have hit the "Pause" button and written down your personal SWOT, it is time to pray and reflect. For some of you this might be an easy thing you currently do. For others, it might seem foreign to you. Regardless, it is never too late to learn how to pray. I pray at least three times a day, in the early morning when I take my dog outside, lunchtime, and before bed.

You can pray whenever, and wherever, you are comfortable. It is not like you have to follow a script or do it perfectly. Do it proud and do it aloud. Thank God for any and all blessings in your life – be specific! Ask God for wisdom in all areas of your life. Talk about specific temptations or challenges you are facing. God has heard it all.

He knows every hair on your head and loves you. Meditation might take the form of quiet time in a peaceful, outdoor area. It might be listening to calming music or tones. It might be through a yoga practice. Prayer and meditation help us refocus and recalibrate our lives. Take the time for yourself. You are worth it.

Be Willing to Fail – Step Outside Your Comfort Zone.

A lot here to digest. "Change or die" as my professor once told me. Life keeps moving so you have to keep moving, too. And I don't know about you, but I would much rather move forward in life than sideways or backwards. Do not be afraid to try new things or to be a different, better person. Failure is part of life. You might not succeed at everything, and that is ok! Do not spend your life playing things conservatively and in a comfort zone. An abundant life is meant to be lived and fully experienced. Do it. God is with you every step of the way. He has made you and shaped you and has given you unique talents and abilities. Use them to serve Him and serve others.

Pareto's 80/20 Principle.

Are you familiar with this? The basic thrust of the 80/20 principle is that 20% of your effort gives you 80% of your results.

Or, think of it in more simplistic terms.

Think of a menu at a restaurant. I bet 80% of the time you only order from 20% of the menu. Think of your wardrobe at home. I bet 80% of the time you gravitate towards wearing 20% of the same shirts, pants, slacks, suits, ties, you own. This principle works because it accurately defines how human nature actually works and how we make selections and choices.

In a town, 80% of the taxes might be paid by 20% of the residents or larger commercial property owners; in a for-profit company, 80% of the revenues might come from 20% of the product line; and in the nonprofit sector, 80% of fundraising dollars raised might come from 20% of the donor base. It is simplistic, and it works. Think about your efforts in your work environment. Make sure you are focusing on things that actually bring results, whether it is revenues, sales, donor dollars, etc. Think about your home life.

Make sure in your marriage you are focusing on the things that are important to your spouse. Think of your spending and investments. Focus on the money matters that bring you the greatest return on investment. Think of your friends and associates. Focus on spending time with those that lift you up and give you the greatest joy and support. By simplifying your choices, and harnessing your efforts, you will see greater results and spend less time choosing and more time doing.

I know this chapter was less spiritual and more practical but when I prayed about the content of this book, I wanted to ensure there were practical tools, like the SWOT analysis and the 80/20 principle, that you could jump right into and apply to your life immediately.

I would be remiss if I didn't end this chapter with several Scripture readings for you to reflect upon. They will help solidify the messages in this chapter and help propel you into Chapter 12 where we will talk about faith and fear.

Psalm 118:24 (my favorite scripture and the first thing I say in the morning when I wake up) – This is the day the Lord has made, let us rejoice and be glad in it.

Matthew 6:6 – But when you pray, go into your room, close the door and pray to your Father, who is unseen. Then your Father, who sees what is done in secret, will reward you.

Matthew 11:28-30 – Come to me, all you who are weary and burdened, and I will give you rest. Take my yoke upon you and learn from me, for I am gentle and humble in heart, and you will find rest for your souls. For my yoke is easy, and my burden is light.

Chapter 12

Faith > Fear

One of the things I learned through my faith journey is many people, even devout Christians, or members of any organized religion, make the mistake of picking and choosing how they apply the tenants of their faith. Some of us will recognize God in our marriages and parenting but not in our workplaces or volunteer endeavors, or vice versa. And sometimes it is not even a question of recognition; we do not apply our faith principles consistently in the different areas, which is even worse.

I know for myself, as a recovering politician, I was good at having faith on Sundays at church but not applying it to my marriage or workplace. I was adept at being manipulative and holier than thou in my political activities, leading from a place of arrogance and self-importance, rather than servant leadership as taught by Jesus.

My message to you is you are either on God's team or you are not. You either have faith and love or you have fear.

You shouldn't look at faith like it is an "a la carte menu" at Ruth's Chris Steak House, although who doesn't love a good ribeye steak now and then? Don't use your faith as a weapon either — well I have it in my marriage to my wife, but boy oh boy I don't see it at my workplace 10 hours a day. I see God in my children but man oh man I can't see it with my spouse. When we pick and choose how we apply our faith we are acting out of fear and not love, and these are the only two emotions to be found. I do not suggest all will be hunky dory and because you walk with Jesus somehow a path of gold will lay before you as you walk through life. Instead, I offer the following advice: you must choose Christian faith in all of your activities, relationships and endeavors. Be committed to something greater than self; acknowledge God's supreme role in your life, whatever your current Christian denomination or however often you attend church. Do not think we are simply here to live a mundane life and pick and choose where we apply faith and where we apply fear. *Make your faith bigger than your fear and persevere.*

Fear is the cheapest room in the house.
I'd like to see you in better living conditions. Hafiz

Let's talk about three (3) key points here:

- ◆ Spiritual identity gives faith

- ◆ Spirituality gives strength, direction, capacity for resiliency due to alignment with spiritual beliefs

- ◆ China/India/US study recently indicated spirituality cuts risk of depression by half

The first point is spiritual identity gives faith. As a Christian, I believe in Jesus and the power of His message. I believe He came from Heaven and lived a pure life and suffered, died, and was resurrected for all of us. My identification as a Christian believer gives me great joy and peace. The Bible and its readings give me the playbook to lead an honorable life. It is my duty, therefore, to be a light and example to others, and to live appropriately. That means at home, at work, and when no one is looking. Not an easy thing to do sometimes as we all face temptations, challenges, hurts, disappointments. I am grateful God is a forgiving God for we are all sinners, right? None of us is perfect. Jesus was perfect, and He died for our sins. That is a powerful reality and message. For me, Christianity is the answer and Jesus is my Lord and Saviour. Christianity gives me faith.

The second point is spirituality gives strength, direction, capacity for resiliency due to alignment with spiritual beliefs. Before I became a born again Christian, I used to think I was the smartest person in the room, and I had all the answers. By reading the first half of this book, you know that not to be true. Now, by waking up every day with Scripture, spending quiet time with God, and having faith, I have an unlimited amount of strength.

It's funny: when I was a kid, I always wanted to be a superhero, immersing myself in dozens of comic books each month as an escape from bullying. Who knew Jesus could be my actual superhero and provide me with the strength and power to save myself and others, too?

Christianity gives me direction and purpose. It is not about me anymore. It is about service to others. Yes, I take care of my basic needs and functions, sure. But once you get the basic stuff out of the way, you realize you have the capacity for way more. Doing for others is so much more fulfilling and rewarding.

We all get so caught up in our view of life, in our minutia, in our toils and tribulations, some of which are really serious. But when you can step away from yourself, and your needs, wants, and problems, and use your Christian faith for points north, it changes everything. It is like when you have children – and I for one am blessed with two great young women as my step-daughters – it becomes more about them and less about you. Well, for you my Christian brothers, it is less about you and more about directing your energy and efforts toward serving others.

Walking with Jesus and the Christian faith gives you the capacity for resiliency. It is like the song from Chumbawamba "Tubthumping" from the album Tubthumper 1997 EMI/Universal. Also known as "I Get Knocked Down" from the song's first line. It was a popular song back in the day, and the constant refrain of "I get knocked down, but I get up again...You are never gonna keep me down" could be an excellent reminder to you for true Christian faith.

We are all going to face challenges in our marriages, with our kids, with our finances, in our careers, and with our health. Some days will seem victorious, others will seem disastrous. The roller coaster of life. Through my life I have had many successes and failures.

The constant for me has been the ability to see obstacles (as noted in the previous chapter) and overcome them. I know too many people in life who, when they hit the wall created by the enemy, they stop. They stare at the wall, lament its presence, and freeze. They no longer make or attempt progress. Christianity is about moving forward.

It is about strapping on the shield and sword and pushing through. It is about finding a different way because Christianity is a different way! It is about going over the wall, under the wall, around the wall, and yes, sometimes just straight through the wall! Do not let the enemy deprive you of attaining your goals and dreams. If you are in alignment with your spiritual faith in Christ, all things are possible.

The final point is actually a validation of the first two. In a 2016 article entitled "Phenotypic Dimensions of Spirituality: Implications for Mental Health in China, India and the United States", authors McClintock, Lau, and Miller showed "those in the top quartile of religious and spiritual commitment compared to all others had approximately half the likelihood of having major depressive disorder, suicidal ideation, and generalized anxiety disorder."

Additionally, the authors state "arguably the most complex of the derived spiritual dimensions, religious and spiritual reflection and commitment involves an orientation of one's life toward a transcendent power.

Whether or not in the context of an established religious tradition, such a commitment inexorably bestows upon an individual a sense of meaning beyond one's own life" (Cloninger, 2006). Special thanks to my friend and mentor, Dr. Thomas C. Barrett, Professor, Psychology and Associate Director for Clinical Training, Psy.D in Counseling Psychology, College of Saint Elizabeth, for providing me with this research.

McClintock, CH, Lau E, and Miller L
(2016) Phenotypic Dimensions of Spirituality: Implications for Mental Health in China, India and the United States. Front. Psychol. 7:1600. Doi: 10.3389/fpsyg.2016.01600
https://www.ncbi.nlm.nih.gov/pmc/articles/PMC5082226/

Did you read what I just wrote? Kudos to the authors for the study – religion and spirituality cut the risk of depression, suicidal thoughts, and anxiety, in HALF. Friends, if a drug company could legitimately make that claim people would be lined up out the door for this magic pill.

It is not magic, it is called faith. Choosing to walk with Jesus can change not just your life, but the lives of those around you. Think of all the people you (we) know who are using prescription medication, or alcohol, or other legal or illegal drugs, to manage anxiety and depression. Think of how different their lives would be if they acted in and with faith and believed in God and a better way. The impact would be huge, and the world would be a better, more spiritually enlightened place for all. **Do not underestimate the impact your faith in Jesus can have on the world at large.**

Now that I have identified the three (3) key points of this important chapter, let's chat about actionable steps on how you can make faith bigger than fear. And just like in the last chapter, I will present these steps followed by Scripture.

Realize you are a child of God.

I don't know about you, but when I see those words, my eyes always begin to well up with tears. It grounds you to understand that in spite of where you are in life, what age, what income, what family or marital circumstances you are dealing with, you are still, and will always be, a child of the highest God.

I am eternally grateful for God the Father and what He has done for me. No matter how happy or sad life gets you, know who you are and whose you are. He loved you first.

Your current Christian denomination doesn't define you.

I was raised as a member of the Catholic church and now attend a Christian Missionary Alliance (CMA) church. I never really understood the different Christian denominations until a few years ago when my wife and I were looking for a new faith home.

I researched the differences between Catholicism, Lutheran, Methodist, Baptist, and so on. But in the end, no matter which denomination of Christianity you choose, believe in God, believe in Jesus His son and the Holy Spirit, and apply the tried and true biblical principles to your life and to those around you.

You are not your title – it is what you do, not who you are.

As a recovering politician, I spent most of my adult life in goal achievement and title attainment. Now, my favorite title is being a good Christian man.

Your work title, which, let's be honest, often defines us as men and is what we tell others we are, is fleeting. I credit Dan Bove and his wise personal counsel on this one as he drove this point home to me several years ago and it has stuck ever since. Your title at work is what you do, not who you are. Remember that.

Nature vs. Nurture.

According to Diane Lang, therapist, educator, life coach and Adjunct Professor at Montclair State University in Montclair, NJ, 50% of life is genetic or nurture; 10% circumstances; and 40% nature which can be re-wired. Lang indicates further it is possible to re-wire your brain and change your thinking. (Russo/Lang Interview October 5, 2018).

We are all born with certain beliefs, gifts, talents. We have a certain DNA and might be predisposed to certain attitudes or behaviors. All true. That is 50% of the life equation. We are all going to deal with unpleasant challenges in life. That is 10% of the life equation. The remaining 40% of the life equation is nature which can be re-wired. Just because you were raised a certain way doesn't mean that has to be your belief system in the future or necessitate a certain response to life's challenges.

It takes time. It takes focus. It takes a faith in something bigger than self, like Jesus. Do not waste your life and the limited time you have on this earth thinking (1) I was raised a certain way and can't change or (2) this situation is so devastating that I can't or won't recover from it. That is all bunk. Do not have a victim attitude. Shift your thinking to God and you will be able to not only survive but thrive. If you have not done this before; if you have found yourself getting knocked down over and over, then maybe it is time to try something different like God?

I hope you found this to be a very intellectually stimulating chapter. I wanted to give you some things to think about with deep clarity and sincerity. I am grateful you took the time to learn more about faith, from my personal spiritual journey perspective, but also from the academic and clinical perspective of people who are experts in the field of psychology. I believe it is time to acknowledge the reality in our dysfunctional world that faith has a true role in making lives better, and rather than running from faith we should run towards it as it has the answers we are looking for. We should stop looking around for magic pills and elixirs, and believing in false Gods such as alcohol, tobacco, drugs, famous athletes or politicians, etc., and have true faith in the power of Scripture and a belief in a loving, gracious God. Choose Christian faith over fear.

2 Corinthians 5:7

For we live by faith, not by sight.

James 2:17

In the same way, faith by itself, if it is not accompanied by action, is dead.

Matthew 5:16

In the same way, let your light shine before others, that they may see your good deeds and glorify your Father in heaven.

Chapter 13

Peace, Purpose, and a Prism

The three P's – say them three times fast! Now that we have learned how to make our faith greater than our fear, we can talk about an even further application of Christian faith that will bring you great joy and lead you to inner peace.

Thus far, I have talked a lot about my journey, my life, toils and tribulations, and how I overcame obstacles to stand before you today, a renewed man of Christian faith. I want to share with you one final thought-provoking point before we wrap it all up in the next chapter with a final path to victory and that is to find your peace and purpose.

Let's take purpose first. For our discussion, purpose is directly related to how you spend your time as a Christian man in the workplace and in volunteer endeavors.

I want you to think about the visual of a colorful prism (depending on your age, thinking about Pink Floyd's *Dark Side of the Moon* album cover is completely appropriate!).

Keep that picture in your head at the moment and let's look at it in greater detail. What do you see on the left side? A single line, a bolt of energy or action, a monochrome color perhaps or none at all?

All would be correct answers. How about in the triangle? Motion, activity, movement, and the line of energy starts to spread, starts to grow. How about on the right side of the triangle? What happens to that single line that entered — well, it spreads dramatically into an abundance of energy and color, right? Think of the single line of entry as the unique purpose God puts inside each of us. Some of us are public speakers, some of us are doctors or nurses or lawyers or accountants. Others teach a craft like plumbing or electrical, others practice these skills. The point is God has placed inside each of you a special talent or skill that is unique to you and cannot be taken away from you. That is your purpose.

Now, how does peace come into play? Well, true inner peace is about recognizing and accepting your purpose and doing something with it. It is about respecting God's wishes for your life and respecting your true inner self.

It is about spreading out into the universe that with which you have been blessed. Take the time to recognize your talents and find a way to make your passion your profession; use your limited time on this earth wisely and <u>make a difference.</u>

I can hear some of you already. *Tom, sounds cool, but what if I have no passions?*

Here are some helpful guides if you find yourself sinking in the boat of uncertainty.

Spend time alone.

I know, hard right? Some of us have a problem being tuned out from the world, away from family & friends, or the electronic devices that are attached to our ears, eyes, wrists, or hips. Time to put the devices down and find some quiet time away from the world where it is just you and God talking. Remember, the trees grow in silence, and so do you.

Reflection.

Ok, now that you are spending time alone (with God of course), take the time to review your daily activities. Are they in spiritual alignment with what God wants for you?

Are you taking it to life or is life taking it to you? Are you genuinely joyful in all of your relationships and activities? It is very difficult, if not impossible, to accurately answer these questions in the middle of work or home life, in the middle of projects or arguments, or in the middle of paying bills online. Take the time, alone, to reflect about who you are and what you are doing and the things you are really passionate about will come to the surface.

Think of the happiest times/moments in your life when time did not matter.

Ok, you are alone with God, you are reflecting, now what specifically should you concentrate on to get the best results? This might be the easiest part. Think about your life, from childhood to present day. What activities and things can you remember doing when time stood still? When you didn't watch the clock all day hoping the dials would move faster than time permitted? When you had genuine joy? Those are your passions. Friends, as men, we get so caught up in this world focusing on titles and income levels and tax brackets that we forget how to be joyful.

I am not talking about happy – buying a watch can make you happy, eating certain foods can make you happy. Happiness in the material world is fleeting, it does not carry through in a permanent fashion. Joy comes from Jesus and is eternal. The goal, therefore, is not happiness, but joy.

When you spend time alone in reflection and think about tasks that bring you joy, those are the things you should be doing with your career and volunteer endeavors. I know too many people who overthink things when the answers are not in front of them, they are deep inside where the Holy Spirit resides. Go deep within and you will find the answers.

Now, on the other side of the spectrum, some of you are saying, *Tom, what if I have **too many** passions?* Friends, I got you covered one way or another here! Let's talk about this challenge on the other side of the passion spectrum.

Can be paralyzing (Paralysis by analysis).

I love many things. I love the New York Rangers hockey club but can't play goalie like King Henrik. I love the New York Football Giants but can't run like Saquon Barkley. I love the New York Yankees and have a great Mizuno first baseman's glove but I do not have Aaron Boone calling me to play first base.

You have to be realistic about what you can monetize and do with your time. Not everything you like to do is meant to be your career. And that is ok. It just means you have some things you are passionate about that are career-worthy, and other things that are just hobbies.

"A ha" Moment.

Not everyone gets hit by a bolt of lightning with the knowledge of their calling. I was fortunate that I knew politics and public service were my career passions early on in life, but I am odd in that regard. It's ok if you have to work through your list of passions.

This isn't the movies where some dramatic John Williams score will be playing in the background and you finally realize you should run a widget factory. Don't expect a singular moment to give you the clarity of purpose you need, it will take time and work, but it is well worth it.

Rank them if you have to.

When you come to the realization you have too many passions or things that interest you, rank them. Establish some sort of list and ranking system so you can effectively focus on the ones at the top of your list. If you focus on too many things, you focus on nothing.

As I said previously, some of the things you list will be career-worthy, and some will be hobbies, while others might be volunteer opportunities in the making.

Talk to Others.

Make three lists of people: those you know really well, those you know somewhat well, and those not at all. We call this step "conducting informational interviews".

If you can write down 5-7 people in each category, that is over 15 people you can reach out to discuss your passions and find out how they do what they do, why they do what they do, and how you can be a part of that career world.

Most people, if they are truly successful in their careers and comfortable in their own skin, will be flattered you want to hear from them about their lives and career decisions. You can find accurate contact information for people you admire online with social media accounts like Facebook, Twitter, and LinkedIn. Take advantage of the low or no cost opportunities to connect with people you admire. Join a local networking group like Kiwanis, Rotary, or chamber of commerce. Sign-up for a men's group at your local church. Don't be afraid to step out of your comfort zone to learn from experts in your field of play.

Be Patient and Be Active.

Thinking about your career and your decisions might be new to you. The steps I have showed you might be difficult at first. Be patient with yourself. Give yourself time. But remember to stay active with this process, too.

No one else in this world will care as much about your education and career decisions as you do, take the time and work through the lists above. You will see results. Faith is great. Faith in action is better.

If you go through these steps, whether you are in the "no passion" group or in the "too many passions" group, here is what you will gain. You will see growth in your career development. You may find you are on the right track with your current position, or you may realize it is time to pursue a different path. When you are in alignment with God's purpose for your life, you will have greater satisfaction and inner peace. This will lead to improvements in your physical and mental health. When your physical and mental health improve, so will your relationships and friendships. Change comes from within.

One of the most important things you will gain in this process is recognition all jobs and volunteer endeavors have value! Read that again: **ALL JOBS AND VOLUNTEER ENDEAVORS HAVE VALUE!**

I don't care if you are the CEO of a Fortune 100 company, a clerk at the local fast food joint, or the janitor at a high school. If you are in alignment with God's purpose for your life, and if you are in a position where you can pursue this passion, then go for it!

And remember, **YOU ARE NOT YOUR TITLE!** It is about the work. It is about having relevancy and impact in this world. Titles come and go. Do not focus on the title of your position. Having a title doesn't make you a leader. Being a leader doesn't require having a title.

Make sure you find your joyful purpose and inner peace. Life is too short to live otherwise.

I hope this career-centric chapter was helpful to you as we tie together faith with action. I have some great Scripture readings for you on peace that will help center you as you go through this process.

In the next chapter, we will tie all of our lessons together, so we can be ready to win. Our journey together is almost over, but your journey has only just begun.

John 16:33

I have told you these things, so that in me you may have peace. In this world you will have trouble. But take heart! I have overcome the world.

Romans 5:1-5

Therefore, since we have been justified through faith, we have peace with God through our Lord Jesus Christ, through whom we have gained access by faith into this grace in which we now stand. And we boast in the hope of the glory of God. Not only so, but we also glory in our sufferings, because we know that suffering produces perseverance; perseverance, character; and character, hope. And hope does not put us to shame, because God's love has been poured out into our hearts through the Holy Spirit, who has been given to us.

Matthew 5:3-5

Blessed are the poor in spirit, for theirs is the kingdom of heaven. Blessed are those who mourn, for they will be comforted. Blessed are the meek, for they will inherit the earth.

Chapter 14

Ready to Win!

Ok friends, we have talked about many things in this book. I have shared intimate details about my life's ups and downs and how I turned the darkness into light when I turned my life over to Jesus. We talked about the positive things that can happen to a man when he finds true Christian faith, and we talked about the lengthy list of negative emotions and activities that can be eliminated or mitigated when faith in God is your moral compass and not yourself. We overcame obstacles, found faith bigger than fear, and found true peace and purpose in the prism of life. Pretty cool stuff. Now, we are ready to win! What do I mean? Let me tell you.

I don't want you to focus too much on your past transgressions, on how life got you down and caused misery in your personal or professional life. We have all been through those challenges; sometimes we succeeded, other times we failed miserably. Remember through Christ all things are possible. Or as Liz Curtis Higgs wrote, "With God, it isn't who you were that matters; it's who you are now in Christ." The purpose of this book was to help you create the best Christian man you can be. God saves. God forgives.

When you can work through your challenges with counseling or mentoring, you will forgive yourself, too.

I am not an expert by any stretch of the imagination. I am just an average guy from New Jersey who had some talent, made some great decisions, and made some stupid ones, too. I know from the bottom of my heart, if I can change, you can, too. I am not going to lie to you and tell you it's easy; it's not. Nothing in life worth having is easy. But I can tell you the rewards in this life, and in the eternal, are well worth it.

To keep with the political theme of the book – you must build a wall between good and evil and make evil pay for it! Pardon the pun, but the reality is the more talent God has given you, and the more success you have in life, the more the enemy will take shots at you. The enemy will devise very creative strategies, both when you are awake and when you are asleep, to get you off of the righteous path God has devised for you.

Unless you spend time in meditation and prayer as I suggested, you will have difficulty resisting the plethora of temptations that will undoubtedly come your way. The trees grow in silence, and your Christian faith needs to do the same.

Don't make the mistake thinking when things are going really well in your marriage, at work, or with your kids, you are safe. No. **It means you are a bigger target for the enemy.**

I know now when I was at my political peak, I thought I was invincible and king of the world. *Au contraire mon frère.* That is when I was most vulnerable to the attack. Protect your flank and stay aware of the world around you. To use Star Wars terminology: the enemy knows the thermal exhaust port flaw in your Death Star and will use every opportunity to shoot at it. This is warfare friends, and we need to win. Failure is not an option. There are too many people counting on you, and me, to be victors, not victims.

As men, we like science fiction stories, heroes, and such. Think of this book as a throw-down challenge. I am challenging you to take the tools, skills, talents and gifts God has given you and spread your light into the world of darkness around you (prism) and be a real super hero. No matter how big or small, every situation offers an opportunity for growth...an opportunity to do the right thing, even if it is difficult or unpopular.

And remember, others will challenge your Christian faith. They will mock it. They will run from it. They will call you judgmental. They may end friendships or relationships with you over it. As Gandhi said, "I will not let anyone walk through my mind with their dirty feet." Let them wallow in their misery; be the beacon of light God intended you to be.

The people who have the greatest difficulty being around and accepting the new and improved version of you might just need your light and positive energy to change their lives. Also, there have been studies that show when people change attitudes or behaviors, it takes a long time for their loved ones to catch up to them as if they are stuck in an older episode of your show while you are already in a new season on Netflix. Be patient and be kind. As long as you are consistent, they will see the changes you made have permanency.

There are only 2 choices in life: fear and love; choose love. In all things. In all situations.

You are never too old to re-create yourself into being the Christian man God wants you to be either. Don't use excuses about time or space, or age or opportunity, to prevent you from becoming the best version of yourself.

Have a personal relationship with Christ – talk to Him! Engage, be purposeful, and intentional. Spread love, peace, hope and joy, the world needs it. The world needs you.

Focus on your goals and work backwards from them. Developing a solid action plan like a Vision Board can help you win. Let's take some time here to delve deeper into what a Vision Board is and how it can help you be hyper-focused.

VISION BOARD

There are two versions of the Vision Board I have used personally with great success over the years.

One is a pictorial representation of the people, places, and things that are important to you, now and in the future. I have seen many people cut images out of magazines, or print them out online, and place them on big poster boards. Most men are visual, so if this describes you, then I suggest getting a good pair of scissors and some tape ready.

The other is a representation of the same people, places, and things, but in an itemized list fashion. I like both choices, but I currently find myself using the itemized list because I am anal retentive and think in a linear, bulleted-list, A-Z fashion. Strange, but it works for me.

Now that I have you jacked up and motivated to create your own version, let me tell you some categories I recommend keeping in mind as you begin.

Spiritual

I think you should start with this category as it emphasizes the pre-eminent role of God in your life. Talk about your spiritual goals as a Christian man: quiet time, Scripture readings, prayer and meditation. Be specific. God should be the foundation in all things you do and all that you are.

Personal

This is where you can get into the relationship with your spouse or significant other. You can talk about your kids, no matter how young or old they are.

How about parents, siblings, or nieces or nephews? I use this category to also talk about the books, movies, and entertainment options I bring into my home and mind. If you are attending church regularly and reading the Bible, but are watching garbage TV or movies, then you are sending your soul very mixed messages. I know we all need mindless activities now and then, just try to minimize them as best you can because if done in greater proportion than the spiritual, they have the ability to drown out the positive Christian messaging with negative thoughts that will provide you the implied justification for negative actions. **Be careful.**

Health

This is where you can talk about your body weight, specific dietary needs you have (gluten-free, low-carb, dairy-free, etc.), exercise, and sleep. Maybe you have certain health challenges you are currently dealing with and you need to be intentional about medication or how to handle them. Don't just say you want to be "healthy" – define what that term means to you.

Wealth

Being specific about your vision and goals is extremely critical here. Are you looking to pay off X dollars in debt?

Are you looking to buy a new home? Is there a vehicle you are looking to purchase with cash? How about investments or pension? Don't forget to prioritize tithing to your local church! People make the mistake of thinking money is evil. It is the LOVE of money that is the root of all evil. You cannot serve God and money. But you should always strive to be a good steward of the resources God has entrusted with you, and to seek other financial opportunities through God's wisdom as appropriate.

Being a good provider is very important to us as men. Here is your opportunity to set specific, measurable goals and intentions, to make this happen. I can't emphasize the importance enough of using a Debt Snowball strategy like the one advocated by Dave Ramsey. Avoid debt at all costs (other than short-term mortgage for your primary residence) as it tends to overpower us and make life very difficult in all facets. And when you struggle with money, you may also find yourself struggling with your faith. Most marriages end in North America because of money issues. Get a grip on your money so it doesn't get a grip on you.

Career/Volunteer

Are you currently in a rewarding position or are you possibly looking to transition? Here is your opportunity to talk about current status and future goals in this regard.

Do you volunteer your time with certain nonprofits or are you looking to expand? If you need guidance on this one, go back to Chapter 13 to review how to find your true purpose in life. Don't just say you want a good career and to volunteer your time. You need to drill down further and be very specific about where you want to work and which organizations you want to give the treasure of your time and talents to.

The Vision Board also presents a nice opportunity to list some Scripture readings or quotes that will keep you focused and motivated during this transformational process. I use Psalm 118:24 on mine and also the aforementioned 80/20 Principle. If you choose to do the pictorial version of the Vision Board, you can cut out pictures of houses, cars, travel destinations, organization logos, etc., to help you stay focused and motivated.

You can put pictures of your spouse, kids, pets, church, favorite vacation spot, and so on. It should not be something a 13-year old would do like gaudy two-tone Swiss watches and exotic cars, or famous people in Hollywood that have nothing to do with real life.

It is meant to be aspirational but faith-centered. And whether you choose to use images from magazines to design your Vision Board, or you list the opportunities, make sure you look at your creation every morning. This will help you set your intention for the day ahead and as men, that is very important for us. I hope this chapter gave you some additional tools and knowledge about how to win. Now, we conclude our journey in the next chapter.

Ephesians 1:18-19

I pray that the eyes of your heart may be enlightened in order that you may know the hope to which he has called you, the riches of his glorious inheritance in his holy people, and his incomparably great power for us who believe.

Deuteronomy 28:1-2

If you fully obey the Lord your God and carefully follow all his commands I give you today, the Lord your God will set you high above all the nations on earth. All these blessings will come on you and accompany you if you obey the Lord your God.

Colossians 3:12-14

Therefore, as God's chosen people, holy and dearly loved, clothe yourselves with compassion, kindness, humility, gentleness and patience. Bear with each other and forgive one another if any of you has a grievance against someone. Forgive as the Lord forgave you. And over all these virtues put on love, which binds them all together in perfect unity.

Chapter 15

A Life Worth Living

Thank you for being a part of this spiritual journey. I hope the initial chapters gave you tremendous insight into not only my childhood and upbringing, but that you would have seen some version of your story in my story. As adults, we are all a product of the good and bad we experienced in our formative years.

The nexus between politics and spirituality, found in the title of this book as well as throughout many of the chapters, is real for me. For you, it might be spirituality and something else. The point I would like you to keep in mind as we conclude our journey together is that spirituality, a true faith in God, needs to be at your core. There will be a plethora of competing interests as you go through life, ones that will take you away from a loving, healthy relationship with the Lord. I cannot stress strongly enough to keep God first. In Chapter 7, I shared intimate details of a man who thought life was no longer worth living; of a person who had it all and couldn't find his way to recognize the gifts given and received. The world has a great way of ruining the purity of purpose given to us by God.

When I hit my lowest moment, some would see that and say how terrible it was. I look back at my fall from grace and realize that was the day God loved me enough to change my life. For that, I am eternally grateful. **Remember, God is more interested in your character than your comfort.**

When I talked to you in Chapter 8 about my faith and how expansive my interests became in the spiritual world, I hope my words gave you a sense of my passion and happiness that came about because of the eye-opening experience of becoming a born again Christian. Hitting the reboot button in life was not just about changing or eliminating bad thoughts, behaviors, and actions, it was about finding the light within so I could share it with those around me. It is hard to be a light for others if you do not do it for you. **Love yourself so you can better love others.**

When we talked about overcoming obstacles, there were many actionable steps which I pray will assist you, because know the challenges and obstacles will always come. It is how we persevere through those challenges that matters. With Christ in your corner, I believe you can maintain a bulldog determination and persistence and focus on your healthy desires. You will find contentment with ambition, and that is a great place to be.

Finally, by overcoming fear and letting faith be your guide, you will find happiness, for you are as happy as you choose to be. Choose love and not fear. Stay close to God, for you are as close to God as you choose to be. If things change, it is because you moved away from Him, not the other way around.

One last thought – I don't know about you, but I like acronyms and "memteks" – memory aids that assist me in trying to remember all of the crazy things I have to keep track of at work and home. I was always this way as a kid, and it hasn't changed. I came up with an easy memtek for you to use so when you face challenges or uncertainty, you have something to refer back to. When life gets you down (and it will) when you are faced with temptations and uncertainty, I want you to **A.C.T. Like a Christian Man** and Find Accountability, Consistency, and Transparency in Your Life.

Accountability

Take responsibility for your words and actions. Yes, we have all been impacted by the world around us. But in the end, you make the determination of what you do and when you do it. Don't lay blame at the feet of others.

Take ownership of what you are and who you are. If you need to change, find a good bible-based church and join, find a men's group and participate, seek good Christian counselors who can walk with you, contact Dan Bove at Pause Ministries in Basking Ridge, NJ and participate in an intensive workshop. Finding male accountability partners at church and through worship, men that can walk with you on the journey of faith, is critical. Men need to be a part of a tribe. There is simply no reason to go through things alone.

Consistency

Make sure the way you are at home is the way you are at work. Don't have different moral standards for different parts of your life, nor for different people you interact with. Staying true to your God-given core in all facets is vital to success. Once you start to deviate in one area, you open yourself up to temptations of the enemy in all areas. Stay on the narrow path. It's easier and it works.

Transparency

Be open and honest. Don't have secrets with your spouse. Share your intimate thoughts and feelings at home.

It's ok to let your loved ones know when you are happy and when you are struggling with something. If you have difficulty being honest with others, you will have difficulty being honest with yourself, and vice versa. Being able to look in the mirror and be true is a very freeing experience. For years, I couldn't look at myself in the mirror without thinking about the hypocrite I was. Be true. Be transparent.

Thank you for joining me on this journey of Christian faith. I hope you follow me on social media and through my website, **nopoliticsinheaven.com.** If I can be a part of your journey going forward and assist you with advice, coaching, and mentoring, please contact me. I would love to hear from you. You are not alone. Lastly, the concluding thought on my Vision Board at home which I see next to me right now, is: ***Happiness is My Default Position.***

With Christ at the center of your life, it is my sincere hope it will be for you, too.

Blessings,
Tom

Acknowledgements

It is an amazing feeling to have finished my first book. There are many people who helped me along the way, not just with this passion project, but life in general. Without them I would not be here. I am sure I will miss some individuals so I apologize for the unintentional slight but as you can imagine, it is difficult to have a brief number of pages with which to thank many who have impacted many decades of one's life.

I thank God every day for saving me and for being the central part of my life and world. Jesus is my Lord and Saviour and I am grateful to walk through life with Him. There is no better friend nor role model than He.

I thank my wife Trish and daughters Ashley and Krista. No three people have impacted me more than them. No three people have supported me more than them. And no three people have seen the changes in my Christian faith more than them. I love you all and thank God for the blessings of three great women in my heart and life.

I thank my parents Tom Sr. and Janet, and sister Lisa, for their love and foundational support over the years. I have also been blessed with many great family members on the Russo, Nobile, and Simos sides; good, solid, ethical people who have been shining examples of God's decency and love.

I am grateful to my childhood friend and editor, Dr. Gordon W. Stables, III, for his support of this project. My life, and this book, would not have been possible without him.

Thank you to Steve Allen, Bill Allmond, Jamie Barberio, Mark Barickman, John Bonanni, Adam Brewer, Clark Brigger, Ed Buzak, Joe Calabrese, Ron Calissi, Sean Canning, Jerry Cerza, Eddie Conrad, Jack Conway, Frank Corrente, Trevor Crane, Dick Cushing, Alex DeCroce, Scott Demarest, Len Deo, Mike dePierro, Wayne Dietz, Joe DiPaolo, Steve Edelstein, Kevin Elvidge, Harry Ettlinger, Russ Fairchild, Greg Fehrenbach, Vinnie Ferrara, Tom Ferry, Tim Fletcher, Dan Flynn, Bob Franks, Dean Gallo, Saul Goodman, Dave Gourley, Dr. Ken Greene, Dr. Matt Hale, Don Hansen, Bruce Hartman, Warren Honeycutt, Louis Karp, Matt Katz, Glenn Kienz, Dr. Robert Kubey, Ed Lally, John Lovell, Henry Luther, Ralph McGrane, Ed Mosberg, Som Mukherjee, Brad Muniz, Baba Oluyemi, Gary Orlando, Rich Phelan, William Primus, Frank Priore, Tom Reilly, Joe Ricciardo, Edward Rochford, John

Rosellini, Mario Rosellini, Jay Ross, Lee Rouson, Glenn Scotland, Michael Shapiro, Bruce Sisler, Bob Springer, Huston Taylor, Mark Taylor, Dominick Tierno, Geoff Urbanik, Dr. Lou Valori, Jim Vigilante, Steve Vorrius, Paul Weiner. I learned a lot about life from these (and other) men. Thank you for being on the train.

Thank you to the following for their advice and support in writing a book as a first-time author: Lorraine Ash, Kirsten Bunch, Katrina Foster, Marissa Haight, Carole Kincaid, Linda Mitchell, Devon Richards, Dhylles Victoria.

I am grateful for the support, knowledge and wisdom of Dr. Thomas Barrett, Lonnie Berger, Dan Bove, Debbie Carcuffe, Bruce Cialfi, Pastor Clyde Cook, Sandra Lee Diglio, Irene Sonja Fanane, Pastor Anne Havrilla, Richard Hawkins-Adams, Pastor Dave Hentschel, Diane Lang, Helen Le Frois, Pastor Frank Leone, Dr. Larry Lincoln, Rev. Msgr. Martin McDonnell, Dr. Alexandra Miller, Dr. Roseanne Mirabella, Dena Moscola, Judge Andrew Napolitano, Terri Oswin, Pastor James Panza, Pastor Frankie Pavia, Pastor Peter Pendell, Dr. Mark Reed, Dr. David Schroeder, Dr. Lori Shemek, Dr. Anne Taylor, Dr. Pannill Taylor, Dr. Glen Wilson, Dr. Jay Wrigley. Thank you for being higher vibration influences.

I am grateful for the inspiring words of Shawn Achor, Adyashanti, Dr. Michael Bernard Beckwith, Pastor A. R. Bernard, Jack Canfield, Dr. Deepak Chopra, Dr. Stephen Covey, Dr. Wayne Dyer, Dr. Tony Evans, Viktor Frankl, Pastor DeVon Franklin, Jon Gordon, Pastor John Hagee, Pastor Matt Hagee, Louise Hay, Dr. David Jeremiah, Laurie Beth Jones, Joseph Juran, Dr. Jack Kornfield, Dalai Lama, Pastor Greg Laurie, Jerry Lewis, Pastor Max Lucado, Pastor Tim Lucas, Pastor Robert Morris, Caroline Myss, Pastor Joel Osteen, Dr. Mehmet Oz, Vilfredo Pareto, Dr. M. Scott Peck, Pastor Wintley Phipps, Dr. Nido Qubein, Dave Ramsey, Dr. Rob Reimer, Tony Robbins, Gordon Robertson, Rev. Pat Robertson, Father Richard Rohr, Pastor Kerry Shook, Dr. Thomas Stanley, Tim Tebow, Eckhart Tolle, Dr. Shefali Tsabary, James Van Praagh, Pastor Rick Warren, Marianne Williamson, Oprah Winfrey, Gary Zukav. Thank you for being inspirational light-workers in all you do and all you are.

Alfie, Cali, Stormy, Joy, Lucky, and numerous fishes. God shows us love through our pets, too.

Made in the
USA
Middletown, DE